PREFACE

Evolutionary taxonomy arose as a result of the influence of the theory of evolution on Linnaean taxonomy. The idea of translating Linnaean taxonomy into a sort of dendrogram of the Animal and Plant Kingdoms was formulated toward the end of the 18th century, well before Charles Darwin's book On the Origin of Species was published.

Evolutionary taxonomy differs from strict pre-Darwinian Linnaean taxonomy (producing orderly lists only), in that it builds evolutionary trees. While in phylogenetic nomenclature each taxon must consist of a single ancestral node and all its descendants, evolutionary taxonomy allows for groups to be excluded from their parent taxa (e.g. dinosaurs are not considered to include birds, but to have given rise to them), thus permitting paraphyletic taxa.

The book *"Taxonomy and Evolution (LSE-05)"* is written especially in question & answer format to provide students the instant gratification of a correct answer. In this book, we have tried to solve all possible questions from the exams' point of view. Solutions of previous years' question papers have also been included to help students to understand the unique examination structure.

We hope that this book would not be only a favourite study material for the students but also can be a nice resource for teaching. An attempt has been carefully made to present this book more useful and meet the requirements and challenges of the course prescribed by Indian Universities. We wish you a successful and rewarding career ahead. Feedback in this regard is solicited.

– GPH Panel of Experts

ACKNOWLEDGEMENTS

Our compliments go to the **GullyBaba Publishing House Pvt. Ltd.,** and its meticulous team who have been enthusiastically working towards the perfection of the book.

Their teamwork, initiative and research have been very encouraging. Had it not been for their unflagging support, this work wouldn't have been possible. The creative freedom provided by them along with their aim of presenting the best to the reader has been a major source of inspiration in this work. Hope that this book would be successful.

– GPH Panel of Experts

PUBLISHER'S NOTE

The present book LSE-07 is targeted for examination purpose as well as enrichment. With the advent of technology and the Internet, there has been no dearth of information available to all; however, finding the relevant and qualitative information, which is focussed, is an uphill task.

We at **GullyBaba Publishing House Pvt. Ltd.,** have taken this step to provide quality material which can accentuate in-depth knowledge about the subject. GPH books are a pioneer in the effort of providing unique and quality material to its readers. With our books, you are sure to attain success by making use of this powerful study material. Provided book is just a reference book based on the syllabus of particular University/Board. For a profound information, see the textbooks recommended by the University/Board.

Our site **gullybaba.com** is a vital resource for your examination. The publisher wishes to acknowledge the significant contribution of the Team Members and our experts in bringing out this publication and highly thankful to Almighty God, without His blessings, this endeavor wouldn't have been successful.

– Publisher

TAXONOMY AND EVOLUTION

LSE-07

For

Bachelor of Sciences (B.Sc)

Useful For

IGNOU, Rai Technology University, KSOU (Karnataka), NIILM University, Bihar University (Muzaffarpur), Nalanda University, Jamia Millia Islamia, Vardhman Mahaveer Open University (Kota), Uttarakhand Open University, Kurukshetra University, Himachal Pradesh University, Seva Sadan's College of Education (Maharashtra), Lalit Narayan Mithila University, Andhra University, Pt. Sunderlal Sharma (Open) University (Bilaspur), Annamalai University, Bangalore University, Bharathiar University, Bharathidasan University, Centre for distance and open learning, Kakatiya University (Andhra Pradesh), KOU (Rajasthan), MPBOU (MP), MDU (Haryana), Punjab University, Tamilnadu Open University, Sri Padmavati Mahila Visvavidyalayam (Andhra Pradesh), Sri Venkateswara University (Andhra Pradesh), UCSDE (Kerala), University of Jammu, YCMOU, Rajasthan University, UPRTOU, Kalyani University, Banaras Hindu University (BHU) and all other Indian Universities.

Closer to Nature   We use Recycled Paper

GULLYBABA PUBLISHING HOUSE PVT. LTD.
ISO 9001 & ISO 14001 CERTIFIED CO.

Published by:

GullyBaba Publishing House Pvt. Ltd.

Regd. Office:
2525/193, 1ˢᵗ Floor, Onkar Nagar-A,
Delhi-110035
(From Kanhaiya Nagar Metro Station Towards
Old Bus Stand)
Ph. 011-27387998, 27384836, 27385249
   +919350849407

Branch Office:
1A/2A, 20, Hari Sadan, Tri Nagar,
Ansari Road, Daryaganj,
New Delhi-110002
Ph. 011-45794768

New Edition

Price:
Author: GullyBaba.Com Panel
ISBN: 978-93-82688-20-4

Copyright© with Publisher

HOME DELIVERY of GPH Books

You can get GPH books by VPP/COD/Speed Post/Courier.
You can order books by Email/SMS/WhatsApp/Call.
For more details, visit gullybaba.com/faq-books.html
Our packaging department usually dispatches the books within 2 days after receiving your order and it takes nearly 5-6 days in postal/courier services to reach your destination.

Note: Selling this book on any online platform like Amazon, Flipkart, Shopclues, Rediff, etc. without prior written permission of the publisher is prohibited and hence any sales by the SELLER will be termed as ILLEGAL SALE of GPH Books which will attract strict legal action against the offender.

CONTENTS

QUESTION PAPERS

CHAPTER-1

Taxonomic Concepts and Their Development

Introduction

Taxonomy is the branch of science deals with the identification, naming and classification of living things. The scientific classification is the arrangement of all plants and animals in their related groups and is known as taxonomy. This chapter deals with concepts, principles and objectives of taxonomy.

Q1. What is the need of classification?

Ans. The scientific practice of identifying, naming and grouping of living organisms is called **classification**. The branches of biology that deal with classification are called **taxonomy** and **systematics**. Taxonomy, as the name indicates, deals with describing and naming organisms while systematics deals with grouping and arranging the described taxa into a hierarchical classification.

Any systematic study on a given plant or animal can be made easier only when the organism is identified as one belonging to a particular group that has some specific characters. The vast number of plant and animal species that have been identified and described, exhibit a great deal of variation in their form, structure, mode of life and various other aspects. Unless the plants and animals are divided into discrete groups based on the differences and similarities between them, it becomes practically impossible to study them.

Classification of organisms is important because of:

- Identification of unknown species.
- Grouping of new organisms with existing ones.
- Assign names to organisms (Nomenclature).
- Provides a common reference for those already identified.
- It the universal language of communication.

Q2. What is taxon? List the main objectives of taxonomy.

Or

Define Taxon. [Dec-2019, Q.No.-1 (b) (i)]

Ans. Taxon is a taxonomic unit, whether named or not: i.e. a population, or group of populations of organisms which are usually inferred to be phylogenetically related and which have characters in common which differentiate (q.v.) the unit (e.g. a geographic population, a genus, a family or an order) from other such units. A taxon (plural taxa) encompasses all included taxa of lower rank (q.v.) and individual organisms defined by the classification scheme such as particular species or class etc.

Objectives of Taxonomy

- To produce a coherent and universal system of classification.
- The main objectives of taxonomy is the learning of kinds of plants and animals on the earth, their names, distinctions, distributions, affinities and habbit characteristics.
- The assemblage of knowledge gained is another objective which is useful for scientists and civilization in general and provide a method of identification and communication.
- To demonstrate the evolutionary implications of plant and animals diversity.
- To provide a scientific latin name of every group of plants and animals in the world both living and fossils.
- To demonstrate the vast diversity of plant world and its relation to man's understanding of evolution.

Q3. Write the principles of taxonomy.

Ans. The classification plays very important role in taxonomy but it is based on certain principles:

- To develop a workable classification which reflects evolutionary relationships and provides identification and nomenclature.
- Hierarchy is established by International Code of Botanical Nomenclature for plants and International Code of Zoological Nomenclature for animals. Categories like species, genera, families and orders are flexible and individually delimited for each group.
- Taxa are based on correlation of characters and discontinuities in variation pattern.
- Constant and must show little environmental variation for delimiting taxa.
- Taxa should be monophyletic.
- Taxonomic treatments should be practical and consistent in their use of various categories.

- Ancestral features and trends of diversity may often be recognised in the structure of living organism. Ancestral organism should be given careful consideration.

- Morphological characters should be given importance as they provide guidance to primitive versus advanced features and aid in developing phylogenetic relationships. Flexibility should be their to modify classification as and when new evidence is available.

- In phenetic taxonomy taxa are organised and classified pon the bases of similarities of the phenotypes of the organism.

- The modern taxonomy includes cladistic taxonomy which involves summarising knowledge about similarities among taxa in terms of a branching diagram called a cladogram depicting the hypothetical evolutionary histories of the organisms.

- Biogeography is also an important part of taxonomy because it analyses the pattern of distribution of organisms and relates these to the systematics of the organisms.

Classification thus enables us to summarise knowledge about the organisms and also saves time and effort for the purpose of classification.

Q4. Write a brief note on history of plant classification.

Ans. Darwin's 'Origin of Species' in 1959 was used for the classification of plants. The history of evolution of plant classification can be broadly divide into two eras namely the pre-evolutionary and post-evolutionary. The pre-evolutionary can be further divided for the sake of better understanding into four sub-divisions.

(1) The Ancient Greeks and Romans: The period of descriptive botany when many important herbals were written by physicians, naturalists and other scholars. The Hippocrates 'The Father of Medicine' in (460-377B.C.) is reputed to have one of Democritus's disciples who found 'Hippocratic School of Medicine' where they studied the causes of disease and a new light was thrown upon the use of herbs. The knowledge of plants was full of superstitions and contributed little to science.

The prodigious activity of Aristotle in (384-323 B.C.) marks the climax of Golden Age of Greece as Aristotle's encyclopedic mind and amount of research accomplished by his predecessors was balanced by extensive acquaintance with every branch of natural history. The plant was integrated thing to Aristotle. The leaves, shoots and roots were not mere appendages of plant but were member of organised thing having its own characteristics.

Theophrastus of Eresus, the 'Father of Botany' in (370-285 B.C.) indicated essential differences between Dicots and Monocots. He classified plants on the basis of form of texture in trees, shrubs, undershrubs and herbs and in animals on the basis of annual, biennial and perinnial. He also differentiated between centripetal (indeterminate) and centrifugal (determinate) inflorescences, recognised differences in ovary position, and in polypetalous and gamopetalous, perigynous and epigynous plants.

Caius Plinius Secundus (23-27 A.D.) mentioned about thosand plants in his 'Historia Naturalis'. It has 37 volumes in which 16 volumes deals with plants having medicinal values, classification, forestry, plant anatomy and horticulture. Plinius classified trees as forest trees, exotic and fruit trees. He classified trees into glandiferous and pitch-bearing. The former includes catkin bearing trees and later mostly conifers.

Pedanios Dioscorides in first century was famous botanist after Theophrastus who brought out' Historia Plantarum'. His principal writings were on medical botany. His chief contribution is 'Meteria Medica' was description of about six hundred species used for medicinal purposes.

The most significant aspect of this period of early Greek Roman naturalists and scholars was that men began to think fundamentally and originally about universe, supernaturalism and mythology were abandoned with logic and at this time scientific foundation to study nature were laid.

(2) The Herbalists: The herbals of Brunfels, Bock, Fuchs and Cordus sometimes referred to as 'German Fathers of Botany' are representatives of this period. Between 1530 and 1536 Otto Brunfelsiusin (1463-1534) published 'Herbal'which gives description of many plants. It was beginning of modern taxonomy. Leonardus Fuch's 'De Historia Striplum'(1542) and Hieronymus Dock's 'Kreuter Buch' (1539). Fuchs was a medical botanist. His idea of flower is similar to Theophrastus. He distinguished two kinds of flowers, the leafy and the capillary but regarded united in flowers like rose. He arranged plants alphabetically by Greek names in De Historia Stripium.

William Turner often called 'Father of English Botany' (1515-1568). He also arranged plants alphabetically and gave English names to many plants and swept out many of old superstitions about plants.

Valerius Cordus in 1561 published herbal of medicinal plants found in Germany and Italy. John Gerard in (1561-1612) published an account of 1033 plant species in 'The Herbal' or General Historia of Plants' in 1597 illustrated with over 1800 wood-cuts of plants.

Caspar Bauhin's 'Phytopinax' described 2700 species beginning with Graminaceae and ends with Papilionaceae. He wrote 'Prodromus Theatri Botanici' in 1620 and 'Pinax Theatri Botanici' in 1623 and utilised 'Binomial System of Nomenclature'.

The ' Doctrine of Signatures' based on features that resembled portions of human body must have been so created for the purpose of furnishing remedies for the ailments. Many plants were given common names that reffered to supposed remedial properties and the origin of many scientific names which are still in use for example the generic name Hepatica, the leaves in that genus resemble the shape of liver and the leaves and remedy and therefore to be remedy for diseases of that organ.

(3) The Transition Period: The transition period from the Renaissance to the Modern period produced by notable workers. Botanists gradually broke away from traditional doctrine of ancients and developed a new system of nomenclature and classification, the arrangement of plant groups in various system.

(4) The Post-Herbal Period: It is difficult to draw a sharp demarcation between the transition period marked with various attempts of classification which were more or less artificial and the modern period which progressed steadily in the development of a system based on natural affinities.

Q5. Give details of history of animal taxonomy.

Ans. Animal taxonomy was started with Aristotle in (384-322B.C.). He studied anatomy, embryology, habit and ecology extensively and said that animals can be classified by their living actions, habits and body parts. His major studies were (1) Distinctios of mandibulate from haustellate types, (2) Winged from wingless forms in insects, (3) Monitoring other animals like birds, fishes and whales. Orders like Coleoptera, Diptera and Psychae were created by him.

The first important work on both animals and plants were done by John Ray in (1627-1705). He followed Aristotle and divided animals with or without blood and further divided by aaray into those with gills and lungs, production of eggs or the living young ones, the possession of broad hooves or narrow claws, existence of two or more incisor teet and so on. He covered entire animal kingdom. His classification was followed as it was logical, practical and easy to follow.

In 18th century Linnaeus and his followers Hartman and kolreuter helped systematics and advanced further. Linnaeus introduced the hierarchial system of classification in animal and plant kingdom and followed four categories of class, order, genus and species for animals. He coined the word Mammalia instead of Quadrupeda in 1758. He was called 'Father of Taxonomy'.

Lamarck divided the animal kingdom into three section on the basis of their mental capacities. He divided animals into four types namely vertebrates, molluscs, arthropods and radiates. He displayed the groups of animals in the form of branching tree which was beginning of use of phylogeny in systematics.

Cuvier in (1769-1832) was critical of Lamarck's evolutionary concept which affected the progress of animal taxonomy during the period. The first of these was 'Von Baer's Law' which states' The younger the embryo the more closely did it resemble other embryos of the same stage of development'. The second explanation was of Ernst Hackel which is known as recapitulation theory or ' Ontogeny repeats phylogeny'. The third theory of evolution was put forward jointly by Darwin and Wallace in 1859 and was supported by Lamarck and Cuvier and supported systematic zoology.

Darwin's idea in 19th century was widely accepted. The naturalists started searching missing links between unconnected taxa and finally reconstructed 'Primitive ancestors'. Phylogenetic trees were proposed by Hackel and large number of species were discovered.

The modern taxonomy came and its development workers realised that Linnean theory was not perfect as it was based on population studies. Mayr considered species as groups of interbreeding natural population which was useful in 'polytypic concept'.

New terms like biosystematics were added now and taxonomists realised the importance of other characters in sound classification for living animals like behaviour, ecology, genetics, zoogeography, physiology and biochemistry. The taxonomy now got new name as 'biological taxonomy' and taxonomists show their dependence on new characteristics in solving species complexes in 1955 and a state of 'Taxonomic explosion' was reached.

The present taxonomy include all available differences and similarities, phylogenetic adaptations, embryological patterns, biological variations, genetical similarity and behavoural characteristics. The general concordance of the data from all such diverse source mutually support the basic validity of scheme of classification.

Q6. Give an account of plant taxonomy in Ancient India.

Ans. The Indian history of botanical science dates back to Vedic period (1500-600 BC).

It started with development of agriculture and when people started cultivation of various food crops. Several technical terms are available about plants parts and their description in the literature of that time. Plants were studied in relation to medicine, agriculture and horticulture. This information is available in 'Ayurveda', 'Charka-Samhita' and 'Sushruta- Samhita'. About 2500 years ago Bhikshu Atreya a well- known teacher at University of Taxila asked his pupil to collect, identify and describe the properties of all plants growing within a distance of four 'Yojanas' of the university. Dignitaries like Dhanvantri, Nagarjun, Agnivesh Jatukarna and Bhela Harita had an intimate knowledge of characteristics of medicinal plants.

The other earlier works dealing with plant life in a scientific manner is 'Vrikshayurveda' compiled by Parashara was there before beginning of the Christian era and was the basis of botanical teachings and medical studies in Ancient India. The book deals with the categorisation, morphology and anatomy of plants, nature and properties of soil, distribution and description of forests in the country. A system of classification based on comparative morphology ofplants is also available in this work. This plant classification was considered more advanced than any other system proposed before 18th century. Many families 'Ganas' are recognised today. The Cruciferae family was called 'Swastikaganiyam' because the arrangement of sepals and petals resembled a 'Swastiks' and flowers were further characterised by a superior ovary, four free sepals, four free petals, six stamens- two of them are shorter and four are longer, two carpels fused and form a two-locular fruit. The present day Cucurbitaceae was called 'Tripusaganiyam' and was characterised by having flowers which were epigynous sometimes bisexual with five sepals, five fused petals, three stamens and a unilocular ovary with three rows of ovules. This proves that Parashara's work was very useful compilation of scientific studies and shows that in India the classification of plants was attempted in that time.

The main aim of GPH book is to provide knowledge as well as good marks in exam.

CHAPTER-2

SYSTEMS OF CLASSIFICATION: PLANTS

INTRODUCTION

The development of angiosperm is a study of sequential events led to various classification from time to time by several botanists. As we know plants are associated with human life and number of plants known to man have increased, it is necessary to organise them and hence classification came into existence. The knowledge of morphology, embryology, palynology, cytology, biochemistry, physiology and phylogeny are added steps in the concept of classification. Thus, classification is the basic method dependent on the various characters of plants and animals.

Q1. Give the historical background, basis of classification and outline of the sexual system of classification.

Ans. Basis of Classification: As we know that there are numerous types of plants in the world. Thus, it is necessary to group them on the basis of their differences and similarities. So plants are arranged according to their rank in this order: Order, Family, Genus and Species for example as shown in the table below:

Table 2.1

Category	Groups
Kingdom	Plantae
Division	Tracheophyta
Class	Angiosperm Gyrnnospenn
Sub-class	Dicotyledon Monocotyledon
Orders	Solanales etc.
Family	Solanaceae etc.
Genus	Solanum etc.
Species	Tuberosurn nigrum
	Individuals

Sexual System or Artificial System of Classification: Carolus Linnaeus in (1707-1778) proposed a system of classification of plants known as Artificial or Sexual system of classification. Linnaeus classified plants on the basis of characters of stamens and carpels. He also took an account of number of stamens and therefore it is also called as numerical classification.

His classes and orders of plants, according to his Systema Sexuale, were never intended to represent natural groups (as opposed to his ordines naturales in his Philosophia Botanica) but only for use in identification. They were used for that purpose well into the nineteenth century. Within each class were several orders. For example Kalmia is classified according to Linnaeus' sexual system in class Decandria, order Monogyna, because it has 10 stamens and one pistil.

The Linnaean classes for plants, in the Sexual System, were:

Class I Monandria - One stamens e.g. *canna, salicornia*

Class II Diandria - Two stamens e.g. *oeea, veronica*

Class III Triandria - Three stamens e.g. many grasses

Class IV Tetrandria - Four stamens e.g. *Protea, Galium*

Class V Pentandria - Five stamens e.g. *Ipomoea, Campanula*

Class VI Hexandria - Six stamens e.g. *Narcissus, Lilium*

Class VII Heptandria - Seven stamens e.g. *Trientalis, Aesculus*

Class VIII Octandria - Eight stamens e.g, *Vaccinium, Dirca*

Class IX Enneandria - Nine stamens e.g. *LaurusB, utomus*

Class X Decandria - Ten stamens e.g. *Rhododendron, Oxalis*

Class XI Dodecandria - Eleven to Nineteen e.g. *Asarum.*

Class XII Icosandria - Twenty or more stamens attached to Calyx e.g. *Opuntia*

Class XIII Polyandria - Twenty or more stamens attached to receptacle e.g. *Tilia, Ranunculus*

Class XIV , Didynamia - 2 stamens short and 2 long, e.g. *Merltho* (Mint)

Class XV Tetradynamia - 2 stamens short and 4 stamens long e.g. *Brassica* (Mustard)

Class XVI Monadelphia - Stamens forming one bundle only, e.g. *Hibiscus*

Class XVII Diadelphia - Stamens forming in 2 bundles, e.g. *Pisurn* (Pea)

Class XVIII Polyadelphia - Stamens forming many bundles, e.g. *Bombrr.*

Class XIX Syngenesia - Anthers are fused but filament are free (Syngenesious condition) e.g. Many composites such as sunflower

Class XX Gynandria - Stamens adnate to the gynoecium e.g. Orchids

Class XXI Monoecia - Plants monoecious Male and Female flowers are borne on the same plant e.g. *Cucurbita, Morus*

Class XXII Dioecia - Plants Dioecious Male and Female flowers are borfie on different plants e.g. Papaya

Class XXIII Polygamia - Plant Polygamous, male female and bisexual flowers are borne on the same plant e.g. Mango

Class XXIV Cryptogamia - Flower concealed e.g. Algae, Lichen, Fungi, Musci (Moss), Filicinae (Fern) etc.

Linnaeus followed Tournefort in the arrangement of plants in classification but used his idea to modify it further. His classification was artificial as he considered only one major character for delimitation of taxa from each other irrespective of their relationship. By using one criterion different families of monocotyledons and dicotyledons have come in one class. Linnaeus artificial system has been followed in order to present a practical and easy method to identify and place all known plants of that period. He never asserted that his system is perfect and natural and pointed out that instead of one, group of characters should be taken into consideration. Linnaeus has contributed excellent knowledge despite several limitations in his system of classification.

Q2. Give the outline of Bentham and Hooker's system of classification. Point out the merits and demerits of the system.

Or

Describe merits and demerits of Bentham and Hooker's classification of seed plants.   **[Dec-2019, Q.No.-5(a)]**

Ans. The most popular natural system of classification based on general principle of Form-relationship was proposed by two British botanists George Bentham(1800-1884) and Sir Joseph Dalton Hooer (1817-1911). Hooker was Director of Royal Botanic Gardens, Kew. Bentham and Hooker published monumental work 'Genera Plantarum' in (1862-1883). This work includes names, accurate description and classification of all seed plants nearly 97,205 species known at that time and 202 families were recognised in this system. The starting family was Ranunculaceae and ending family was Poaceae.

The basis of classification is given below:

(1) Phanerogams: Flowering or seed plants- classified in 3 classes namely: Dicotyledons, Gymnosperms and Monocotyledons- Based on the division of reticulate vs parallel venation, 4-5 vs merous flowers, 2 vs 1 cotyledon in seed of dicotyledons and monocotyledons resp. Gymnosperms are placed in between dicots and monocots as they bear nacked seeds.

(2) Dicots are further divided in 3 sub-classes:

   (i)   Polypetalae

   (ii) Gamopetalae

   (iii) Monochlamydeae

This division is based on the presence or absence of petals and their fusion.

(3) Polypetalae is further classified into 3 series.

   (i)   Thalamiflorae

   (ii) Disciflorae

   (iii) Calyciflorae

The splitting is mainly based on the position of ovary in relation to thalamus.

(4) Thalamiflorae has 6 Cohort. The starting order is Ranales and Ranunculaceae as the first family. The last or the sixth order is Malvales with Tiliaceae as the last family of the series.

(5) Disciflorae which possess a well developed disc with superior ovary has 4 orders and Umbellales and last family is a anamolous order namely Ordines Anomali is ending orderand Moringaceae as the last family.

(6) In **Calyciflorae** perigynous or epigynous flowers are found which have 5 orders and 27 families. The starting order being Rosales and Connaraceae as starting family and last order is Umbellales and last family is Cornaceae.

(7) Gamopetalae is sub-class where petals are fused and divided into 3 series namely:

(i)   Inferae

(ii) Heteromerae

(iii) Bicarpellatae

This spilliting is based on number and position of carpels. In Inferae the bicarpellary, syncarpous and inferior ovary is present while in the case of Heteromerae, carpels are more than 2 and in Bicarpellate, it is bicarpellary, syncarpous with superior ovary. The number of order in Gamopetalae is 10, 3 in Inferae, 3 in Heteromerae and 4 in Bicarpellatae. There are 45 families, 9 in Inferae, 12 in Heteromerae and 24 in Bicarpellatae.

(8) Inferae has 3 orders namely:

(i)   Rubiales

(ii) Asterales

(iii) Campanulales

The starting family is Caprifoliaceae and last family is Campanulaceae.

(9) Heteromerae also has 3 orders namely:

(i)   Ericales

(ii) Primulates

(iii) Ebenales

The starting family is Vacciniaceae and last family is Styraceae.

(10) Bicarpellatae has 4 orders namely:

(i)   Gentianales
(ii) Polemoniales
(iii) Personales
(iv) Lamiales

The first two orders have actinimorphic flowers while last two have zygomorphic flowers. The starting family is Oleaceae and last family is Labiatae or Lamiaceae. The family Plantaginaceae has been under Ordines Anomali.

(11) The sub-class Monochlamydaceae is divided into 7 series and one series as Ordines Anomali. The starting family being Curvembryeae with Nyctaginaceae and last being Ordines Anomali with Ceratophyllaceae, a hydrophytic family.

(12) The class Gymnospermae is placed between Dicots and Monocots with 3 families namely:

(i)   Cyadaceae
(ii) Coniferae
(iii) Gnetaceae

(13) The class Monocotyledons is divided into 7 series. The starting family is Microspermae with Hydrocharitaceae. The family Orchidaceae is included in this series. The last series being Glumaceae with Gramineae as last family.

Merits: The merits of the above system are:

(1) The observation made from living specimens or herbarium set a standard for generic description.

(2) It is easy to identify plants upto family level.

(3) The geographical distribution of genera is given in the system.

(4) It gives upto date information which is given in the Index Kewensis and update regularly every 5 years.

(5) Although the system is not phylogenetic but position of Ranales is according to the modern concept of evoluation.

(6) The position of Monocots after Dicots is logical and in accordance with the modern concept of evolutionary trends.

Demerits: The demerits of the system are:

(1) The position of Gymnospermae in between Dicot and Monocots is not logical.

(2) The establishment and demarcation of Polypetalae and Gamopetalae as natural groups creates confusion sometimes for example Cucurbitaceae have gamopetalous conditions but Cucurbitaceae has been placed in Polypetalae. In the treatment of Gamopetalae, Asteraceae the highest evolved family has been placed in the beginning of the group and thus the position of Asteraceae is not justified as per evolutionary trends.

(3) The Monochlamydeae as a separate and reduced group is not logical as related families such as Chenopodiaceae could not be place near Caryophyllaceae.

(4) The inclusion of Orchidaceae in Microspermae, the starting series of Monocot is not in accordance with recent evolutionary trends. The Orchidaceae is considered as one of the highest families in monocots and should not be placed in starting family.

Q3. What is phylogenetic systems of classification and what is the basis of Engler and Prantl's system.

Or

Difference between artificial and phylogenetic classification of plants.

Ans. In phylogenetic system the plants are classified according to evolutionary relationship but it is not authentic due to incomplete fossil records and plants are classified on the available data.

Engler and Prantl published a monumental work 'Die-Nuturlichen Pflanzenfamilien' in (1887-1915) having 23 volumes. The basis of this classification states that unisexual,nacked flowers arranged in Catkin and wind pollinated were considered as the lowest grade of floral organisation by Engler as such is called Englerian concept. The next stage of evolution of flower is followed by appearance of 1-seriate perianth leading to 2-seriate condition alongwith bisexual condition.

The outline basis of Engler and Prantl's system is given below:

(1) Plant kingdom has been divided into XIII divisions but after modification by Melchior the total divisions are XVI.

(2) Divisions I-XII are dealing with Bacteria, Algae, Fungi, Bryophytes and Pteridophytes.

(3) The XIII division is Embryophyta Siphonogamia. It is divided into 2 sub-division based on the naked and enclosed ovules namely:

    (i)   Gymnospermae (naked ovules)

    (ii) Angiospermae (enclosed ovules)

(4) The sub-division Gymnospermae has been divided into 7 orders, starting one is Cycadofilicales and last is Gnetales.

(5) The sub-division Angiospermae has been splitted into two

    (i)   Monocotyledonae

    (ii) Dicotyledonae

The division is based on the differences between Dicots and Monocots as venation of leaf, 3-merous flowers in monocots and 4-5 merous flowers in dicots.

(6) Monocots are further divided into 11 orders and 45 families and after modification 14 orders and 53 families. The starting order is Pandanales possess nsaked, unisexual flowers with Typhaceae as starting family. The last order is Microspermae with Orchidaceae.

(7) Dicots are divided into 2 sub-class namely:

    (i)   Archichlamydeae

    (ii) Sympetalae

This division is based on the condition of perianth, 1-seriate or 2-seriate and their fusion for example in Archichlamydeae the flowers may be nacked or 1-seriate followed by 2-seriate condition but the petals aremostly free having polypetalous condition. In Sympetalae the petals are fused and gamopetalous.

(8) Archichlamydeae has 33 orders and 206 families and after modification there are 37 orders and 227 families. The starting order is Verticillatae and Casuarinaceae as starting family followed by order and families with or reduced perianth, 1-seriate or 2-seriate perianth. The last order being Umbelliflorae with Cornaceae as last family.

(9) Sympetalae also known as Metachlamydeae has 11 orders with 52 families and after modification it has 11 orders and 64 families. The starting Order is Ericales and family is Clethraceae and ending order is Sympetalae is Campanulales with Asteraceae or Compositae as the last family which is considered as highest evolved dicot family.

Q4. Give the merits and demerits of Engler and Prantl and Hutchinson's system of classification.

Ans. Engler and Prantl

Merit

- The arrangement of Order and Families in the system is according to evolutionary Tendencies.
- The system provides modern keys for identification of each group of plant.
- The position of Gymnosperms before Angiosperm is accurate and according to Modern concept of evolution.
- The position of Asteraceae as ending Family of dicots is justified.
- The position of Orchidaceae as ending Family of monocot is justified.
- Anatomical data is considered in classification.

Demerits

- The concept of primitive flower is against the modern concept of evolution.
- Monocots are regarded more primitive than dicots.
- Amalgamation of Apetalous with polypetalous families to form Archichlamydeae is not desirable.

- The system is not practical.

Hutchinson's

Merits

- The standard of family description is of high order and valuable features are given in the keys for identification.
- The system of classification is of much practical value.
- The treatment of monocot is more adequate, logical and acceptable.
- The data from floral anatomy and embryology are considered in classification of monocots and dicots
- Geographical distribution of most Genera is included in the system.
- The classification is phylogenetic one.

Demerits

- More stress is given on monophyletic origin of Angiosperm from hypothetical proangiosperm.
- Due to emphasis on Herbaceae and Lignosae, some closely related families have been put apart.

Q5. How many phyletic dicta Hutchinson's system of classification is based? On the basis of dicta, give an outline basis of the classification.

Ans. Hutchinson proposed 24 dicta or principle for his classification and published a book 'The families of flowering plants' in (1926-1934). The volume 1 deals with dicots and volume 2 with monocots. The book was revised in 1959 and the recent one was modified in 1973.

Based on 24 dicta, Hutchinson proposed phylogenetic system of classification. The outline is given below:

(1) Hutchinson brelieved in Monophyletic origin of Angiosperm from a hypothetical group which he named as Proangiosperms.

(2) He divided development of dicots into two namely:

(i) Lignosae (woody)

(ii) Herbaceae (herbaceous)

(3) Lignosae has 54 orders 251 families. The starting order is Magnoliales and family is Magnoliaceae passing through Annonales, Rosales, Malvales, Rubiales and last is Verbenales with Phrymaceae as terminating family.

(4) Herbaceae has 28 orders and 100 families. The starting order is Ranales with Paeoniaceae as starting family passing through Rhoedales, Caryophyllales, Umbellales, Asterales and last is Lamiales terminating family is Lamiaceae.

(5) The monocots have 29 orders and 69 families. Monocots are sub-divided into 3 groups based on the nature of perianth namely:

(i)   Calyciferae

(ii) Corolliferae

(iii) Glumiflorae

The starting order of Calyciferae is Butomales with Butomaceae as starting family and the ending order is Zingiberales with Marantaceae as last family.

The Corolliferae has starting order as Liliales and Liliaceae as starting family. The last order is Orchidales and terminating family is Orchidaceae.

The Glumiflorae has starting order as Juncales and Juncaceae as starting family. The last order is Graminales and Gramineae as terminating family.

The outline of Monocots can represented as given below:

Verbenales	Lamiales	Graminales
Rubiales	Solanales	Cyperales
Glumiflorae	Apocynales	Asterales
Juncales	Malvales	Umbellales
Orchidales	Legumnales	Liliales
Corolliferae	Rosales	Caryophyllales

Zingiberales   Annonales   Brassicales

Alismatales   Calyciferae   Magnoliales

Ranales   Butomales

Q6. Give the outline of Takhtajan's system of classification in the form of a chart.

Ans. Takhtajan, a Russian Palaeobotanist proposed another phytogenetic system of classification in 1942 based on the structural types of gynoecium and placentation. He modified and english version was published in 1958. He coined two terms in his system of classification as:

- Magnoliophyta (Angiosperms)
- Magnoliopsida (Dicots). This was considered as primitive group than Liliopsida (Monocots).

The outline system is represented in the form of Table below:

Table 2.2: Magnoliophyta (Angiosperm)

Magnoliopsida (Dicots) 342 Families	Liliopsida (Monocots) 77 Families
(I) Magnolidae Magnoliales(starting order) Magnoliaceae(starting family)	(I) Alismatidae Alismatales (starting order) Butominaceae (starting family)
(II) Ranunculidae Ranunculales	(II) Lilidae Triuridales Orchidale Poales
(III) Hamamelidae Trochodendrales	(III) Arecidae Arales (21st last order) Arecaceae(77th last family)
(IV) Caryophyllidae Caryophyllales	
(V) Dilleniidae Dilleniales	
(VI) Rosidae Rosales	
(VII) Asteridae Asterales (71st terminating order) Asteraceae (342nd last family.	

Takhtajan accepted main divisions and sub-divisions as classes and sub-classes similar to Bentham and Hookar classification. Further sub-grouping like in families Thalimiflorae, Disciflorae and Calyciflorae only one character is chosen as basic criterion to make it more artificial and Takhtajan modified at this point and on critical examination on the basis of merit, he made use of maximum data available on morphology, cytology, palynology, anatomy, embryology cytogenetics, biochemistry and palaeobotany in construction of taxa of various ranks.

CHAPTER-3

Systems of Classification: Animals

Introduction

Animal diversity is complex and requires an ability to recognise similarities and differences among organism. Classification has 4 important roles to play. The first role is to group animals into categories according to their characteristics. Second, classification helps in improving our predictive powers. Third, classification improves our explanatory power about relationships among animals. The animals are named according to binomial nomenclature, there are two types of names, scientific names and common names.

Classification systems are based on features whose utility depend on what we hope to accomplish with the system. It is based on type of reproduction, habitat and mode of life useful for people to evolve classification of animals.

Q1. Explain the types of classification.

Ans. There are many biological classification of animals but they belong to the following types:

- **Phenetic Classification:** The taxa are based on few characters but in phenetic approach it demonstrates a false claim in establishing natural groups as product of human mind rather than evolution. It is well recognised fact for all natural taxa, especially species with their reproductive isolation, that they are not an arbitrary, subjective and man-made phenomenon. This approach is useful for groups with immature classification and those with non-redundant characters.

- **Natural Classification:** This classification is based on natural characters of the taxa. This is considered as a phylogenetic one reflecting the evolutionary relationships. The animals are placed into many groups and sub-groups on the basis of similarities and dissimilarities. In natural classification, the groups are recognised by having a maximum number of attributes in common with limits set for correlation of other features.

- **Phylogenetic Classification:** It is also called as Cladistic classification. Phylogeny plays a great role in classification as it gives theoretical background for taxonomy and explains all the association involved in the classification. Some people believe that phylogenetic and evolutionary classifications are similar as both based on features derived from common ancestors. Cladistic classification is based on phylogenetic branches as shown in the figure below. But till date there is no phylogenetic classification for animals except that of horses. This is due to incomplete fossil record and other information fail to give clear genealogy.

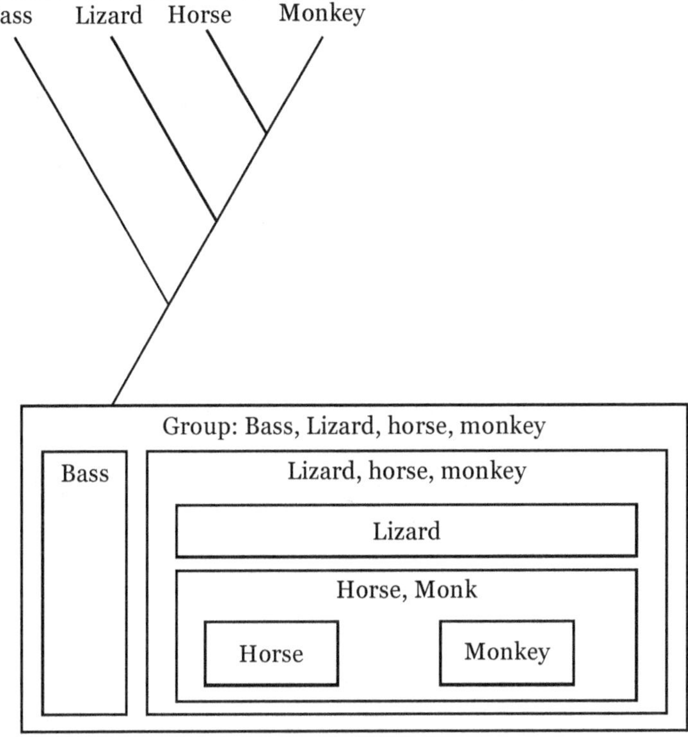

Fig. 3.1

- **Evolutionary Classification:** This classification combines both the aspects of Phenetic and Cladistic systematics. This classification show evolutionary relationship and degree of similarity among organism. It is impossible to represent similarities and genealogies in single classification as evolution among groups and traits within groups of organism are often variable. The evolutionary taxonomists must compromise between their two goals so that users should know how taxonomic categories were constructed. To consider a real example, consider the classification of Pheasants and their relatives. The phasinoid birds are intensively studied in terms of gross morphology. The birds having structural genes for lysozyme C, birds with three different 'α like globins' and those for four 'β like globins'. Each of these are located on different chromosomes. A phenogram for phasianoid birds based on genetic information which can be converted into cladogram if we assume constant rates of evolutionary changes in globin molecules. The genetic evidence is compelling as extent of differences in three gene regions are roughly same in the birds.

Most commonly used classification is Evolutionary one as it is familiar.for example crocodiles are grouped with reptiles because of tbeir morphological similarities with lizards even though they share more recent ancestry with birds than reptiles and in Cladistic classification crocodiles will be grouped with birds rather than reptiles.

- **Omnispective Classification:** This is the extension of the concept of natural classification put forward by Welder in (1967). The approach seems quite realistic and pragmatic. An experienced taxonomist includes all the readily available features of the organism but only those are used for classificaton purposes, which are helpful in estabilishing groupings and distinctions. This practice is used by most of the animal taxonomists.

Q2. What do you mean by taxonomic characters and how their selection is made?

Ans. Classification is done on the basis of information collected on organism and their characters. The characteristics of organisms have been measured on the description of species based on morphology. The morphology can be revealed from fossils or from ancestors of the species. Sometimes similarities are revealed at early development stage but are lost by the time adulthood is reached. The German ethologist Konard Lorenz showed behaviour patterns supported other evidence in ducks that can cross and produce fertile hybrid offsprings showing them genetically similar. The sequence of amino acid in proteins provides information of similarities and differences. The important taxonomic character is the structure of genes themselves, the nucleotide sequences. The most important is cleavage of DNA and RNA by use of enzymes which recognise specific nucleotide sequence helpful in considering the taxonomic characters.

Selection of taxonomic characters: The taxonomic characters useful for classification of organism must be measurable, describable and relatively invariable regardless of environment where they grow. For example leaves have different shapes depending on whether they grow in water or in air. Flowering plants offer branching patterns, leaf shapes, specialised cells, reproductive structures etc. Many invertebrates have shells that readily preserved as fossils and can only be measured after the death of an animal. Thus taxonomic character is a feature present in all appropriate specimens and appropriate time. Only those characters should be selected which are stable within species or group, easily studied and distinctive from other closely related taxa. Thus, the taxonomist has to search good characters keeping in mind that characters should not show wide variation and are easy to distinct and separate from other taxa. The characters should not be influenced by the environment and must be consistent and easily seen in the specimen.

The important criteria in selecting character are its analogy or homology with characters of the organs. Homology is correspondence between two structure due to inheritance from common ancestor. For example the leaves of a vascular plant show modifications but they are homologies of one another. Another example is forelimbs of horses, bats whales and human have same framework of bone structure yet function differently.

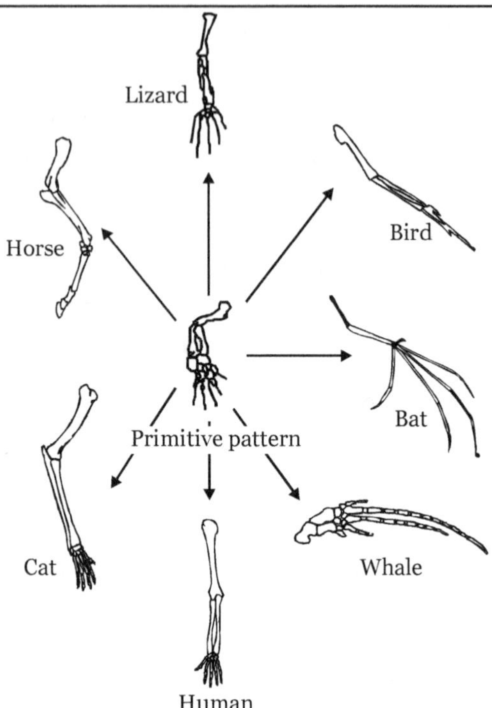

Fig. 3.2

When structures do not come from common ancestry converge to become more similar in functions called analogy and structures are said to analogous. For example wings of butterfly and birds function as flight organs but do not have common origin. These type of structures pose problem for taxonomists as similarities suggest common ancestry but careful study is required to ascertain the original structure actually modified.

Q3. What is taxonomic hierarchy? Make a table to show hierarchy giving example of plant and animal classification.

Or

Write a short note on Taxonomic hierarchy.

[Dec-2019, Q.No.-6 (a)]

Ans. The orderly system of arrangement of organism is called taxonomic hierarchy. It enables us to distinguish clearly between different types of organisms. It also allows us to name about two million known species of living organisms and their extinct ancestors. Each species is assigned two names, one identifies species and other genus to which species belongs and this is known as binomial nomenclature. For example Formicidae is a family which contains all Ant species. Similarily, Homindia is based on Homo families Homoindiae which in turn grouped into orders, orders into classes, classes into phyla and division into kingdom. This various units of classification in order is called taxonomic hierarchy. To understand see table below:

Table 3.1: Examples of Animal and Plant Classification

Taxonomic Group	Animal Examples		Plant Example
Kingdom	Animal	Animal	Plant
Phylum	Annelida	Chordata	Tracheophyta
Class	Oligochaeta	Mammalia	Angiospermae
Order	Terricolae	Primates	Ranales
Family	Lumbricidae	Hominidae	Ranunculaceae
Genus	Lumbricus	Homo	Ranunculus
Species	L.terrestris	H. sapiens	R. acris
Common name	Earth worm	Human	Meadow buttercup

Q4. Explain briefly the five plant kingdom and give their characteristics.

Or

Describe main problems in having two kingdoms of living organisms.

Or

What are the five kingdoms into which living beings are divided? Which group of living being is out of this classification?

Ans. The five kingdoms of living beings are the kingdom Monera, the kingdom Protista, the kingdom Fungi, the kingdom Plantae and the kingdom Animalia.

Viruses are out of this classification and sometimes they are said to belong to their own kingdom, the kingdom Virus.

 Taxonomy and Evolution [LSE-07]

Earlier living organisms were divided into two kingdoms i.e. The Animal and Plant kingdom. The animal kingdom contained organisms which fed heterotrophically and motile and in plants static organisms which fed autotrophically by photosynthesis. The unicellular heterotrophs were put in animal kingdom and unicellular autrophs in plant kingdom with algae. Fungi were regarded as plants which have no chlorophyll and have heterotrophic mode of nutrition. Bacteria was also under plant kingdom because they possessed a cell wall.

The three main problems with two kingdoms. First problem is with unicellular flagellates like Euglena species which were put with protozoa in animal kingdom though some of them contain chlorophyll and feed autotrophically by photosynthesis.

The second problem was with Fungi because fungal hyphae bear superficial resemblance to the filaments of simple multicellular algae like Spirogyra though fungi are different from green plants, not only that they lack chlorophyll and feed heterotrophically but in structure also.

The third problem is with Bacteria when seen through electronic microscope, they have simple prokaryotic cell structure which is shown by blue-green algae. These structure appear similar to each other but different from other eucaryotic organism. Hence five kingdom system was proposed as shown briefly in the table below.

Q5. Give an account of the "Five Kingdom System of Classification" as proposed by Whittaker and mention merits and demerits of system.

Or

Write a note on Five Kingdom Classfication.

[June-2019, Q.No.-2 (b) (i)]

Or

Name Whittaker's five kingdoms of organisms and list their characteristics. **[Dec-2019, Q.No.-3 (a)]**

Ans. The five kingdom system classification was proposed by R. H. Whittaker in 1969 which divides living organisms into five kingdoms.the heterotrophically, the plant kingdom for multicellular motile organisms feed by photosynthesis. The protozoa and unicellular algae are kept in separate kingdom and protista kingdom and bacteria with blue-green algae are unique and are prokaryotic and are combined in Monera kingdom as shown in the figure below. Though this classification solve many problems but also creates some. For example separating the unicellular algae from the simpler multicellular algae is not is not clear as they have certain common features. Therefore it was suggested that all algae, uni- or multicellular should be in Protista kingdom. Some complex organisms like seaweeds are also included in Protista as they are associated with unicellular organisms. Some biologists suggested that they should be called as Prptocista. Whittaker's original five kingdom system has certain advantages but viruses are not dealt here in this system.

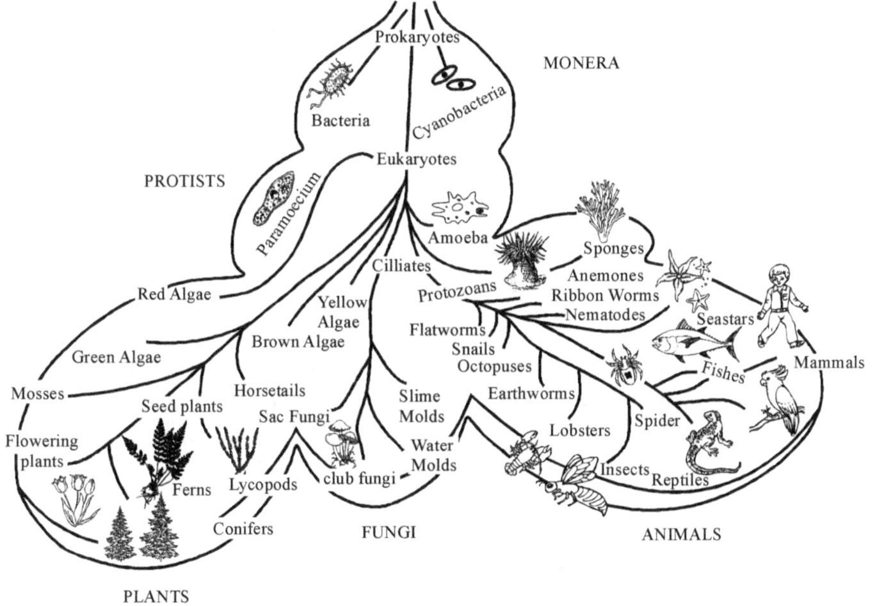

Fig. 3.3

Merits:

- This system of classification is more scientific and natural.

- It is the most accepted system of modern classification as the different groups of animals are placed phylogenetically.
- The prokaryotes are placed in a separate kingdom as they differ from all other organisms in their organization.
- As the unicellular organisms are placed under the kingdom protista, it has solved many problem related to the position of organisms like euglena.
- The fungi totally differ from other primitive eukarytotes hence, placing the group fungi in a status of kingdom is justifiable.
- The kingdom Plantae and Animalia shows the phylogeny of different life styles, in the five kingdom classification, they are more homogeneous group than the two kingdom classification.
- This system of classification clearly indicates cellular organization and modes of nutrition, the character which have appeared very early in the evolution of life. .

Demerits are that in grouping living things into kingdoms, there bound to be anomalies, whatever scheme one adopts. According to figure kingdoms are trunk and main branches are evolutionary tree. Splitting the tree into kingdoms is a arbitrary process.

- This system of classification has drawbacks with reference to the lower forms of life.
- The Kingdom of Monerans and the Protists include diverse, heterogenous forms of life. In both the kingdoms there are autoptrophic and hetertrophic organisms. They also include organisms which have cells with cell wall and cells without cell wall.
- All the organisms of these three kingdoms do not originate from a single ancestor.
- Organisms like the unicelluar green algae like volvox and chlamydomonas have not been included under the Kingdom Protista because of their resemblance to other greeen algae.

- The general organizations of the slime moulds are completely different from the members of protists.
- Multicellular organisms have originated from protists several times.
- In this system of classification viruses have not been given proper place.

Q6. Give an account of protostomes and deuterostomes.

Ans. On the basis of embryonic development, metazoans are divided into Protostomia and Deuterostomia. Protostomes are primitive invertebrates while deuterostomes include echinoderms and chordates. This division helps in understanding relationships of different groups of animals.

Protostomes:

- Protostomes include flat worms, annelids, arthropods, molluscs and some minor phyla.
- During embryonic development blastopore forms the mouth on the anterior end and anus appears later to complete the alimentary canal.
- Nerve cord is ventral in protostomes.
- Fate of blastomeres is determined very early during holoblastic cleavage. This is called determinate cleavage, which means blastomeres are destined to form a particular organ in very early stage of cleavage.
- Cleavage is spiral in protostomes, i.e. axis of cleavage plane is oblique, so that blastomeres have a spiral arrangement in which one tier of cells alternates with the next tier of cells. This is also called mosaic cleavage.
- Mesodermal tissue is formed by the division of a single blastomere 4d cell.
- Origin of coelom takes place by schizocoely by splitting of the mesodermal cell mass.

Deuterostomes:

- Nerve cord is dorsal in deuterostomes.

- Deuterostomes include echinoderms, chordates, pogonophora, hemichordates and some minor phyla.
- Blastopore forms anus during embryonic development and represents the posterior end of body. Mouth is formed later.
- Cleavage is indeterminate and if blastomeres are separated at 4 cell stage, each one will develop into a complete individual.
- Cleavage is radial, in which the cleavage plane is either parallel or at right angle to the polar axis. Blastomeres are arranged directly above or below one another. This is also called regulative cleavage.
- Mesodermal tissue is formed by the outgrowth of endodermal wall of the archenteron.
- Coelom is formed by enterocoely or outpouching of the archenteron.

CHAPTER-4

BINOMIAL NOMENCLATURE

INTRODUCTION

Nomenclature is defined as system of naming objects like here it is objects of biological origin. The binomial system of nomenclature was introduced by Linnaeus in 1753 in his publication 'Species plantarum' in which plant consists of two Latin names. The first is genetic epithet represent Genus and second specific epithet representing Species for example the botanical name of mango is *Mangifera indica* where *Mangifera* is genus and *indica* is species. The scientific names are written in italics and genus always start with capital letter and species with small letter for identification. There is always one scientific or biological name for one organism.

Q1. Explain why the field of biology is ever changing unlike other branches of science.

Ans. The biology field is ever changing with all its contents related to characters, circumscriptions and knowledge etc. Because it is dependent on the scientific findings of related science like morphology, anatomy, embryology and cytology. It is important to mention that international codes have no hand in scientific interpretation but whichever decision or code is followed must guide as to which name or names are to be applied to the entities under study.

Q2. Write a brief note on Development of Concepts of naming.

Ans. The concept of naming originates from its importance and to overcome deficiencies and uncertainties arises from the use of local expression and to give technical designation or scientific names to the organisms. As the biologists disussed the issue, the concept of code of nomenclature developed which is based on the universal set of rules to govern the application of names of biological organisms. Name is a conventional tool to act as reference for example when we say, chimpanzee, sparrow, paddy, virus, we mean to say certain animal, plant or virus as names. There are two trends in naming animals, one is common name and other is scientific name.

Common or vernacular names are convenient in particular region but differ from country to country. These are applied arbitrarily and have no indicated relationship between organisation. Tamla is a flowering evergreen tree and commonly known as Dample, Otor and in Hindi Tamla, paddy is known as chawal in some region, dhan in some and nellu in Madras but uniform scientific name is *Oryza sativa*. So, advantage of scientific name is its definiteness as compared to varieties found in common names.

Q3. What is meant by binomial nomenclature and what are its basic rules?

Ans. Binomial nomenclature (also called binominal nomenclature or binary nomenclature) is a formal system of naming organism of living things by giving each a name composed of two parts, both of which use Latin grammatical forms, although they can be based on words from other languages. Such a name is called a binomial name (which may be shortened to just "binomial"), a binomen or a scientific name; more informally it is also called a Latin name. The first part of the name identifies the genus to which the species belongs; the second part identifies the species within the genus. For example, humans belong to the genus *Homo* and within this genus to the species *Homo sapiens*. The formal introduction of this system of naming species is credited to Swedish natural scientist Carl Linnaeus, effectively beginning with his work *Species Plantarum* in 1753.

The concept originates from its importance so as to overcome the deficiency and uncertainties arising from local expressions. As communication increased among biologists the concept of codes of nomenclature developed on the basis universal set of rules.

The application of binomial nomenclature is now governed by various internationally agreed codes of rules, of which the two most important are the International Code of Zoological Nomenclature (ICZN) for animals and the International Code of Nomenclature for algae, fungi, and plants (ICN) for plants. Although the general principles underlying binomial nomenclature are common to these two codes, there are some differences, both in the terminology they use and in their precise rules.

In modern usage, the first letter of the first part of the name, the genus, is always capitalized in writing, while that of the second part is not, even when derived from a proper noun such as the name of a person or place. Similarly, both parts are italicized when a binomial name occurs in normal text. Thus the binomial name of the annual phlox (named after botanist Thomas Drummond) is now written as *Phlox drummondii* Scientific nomenclature of a species must have, at least, two names: one that classifies it as genus and the other that identifies it as species. The name related to genus is the first and must begin in uppercase, the other following names must be written in lowercase. Besides this rule, scientific names of species must stand out and be written either in italics or underlined or bold or between quotation marks. For example, the scientific name of the human species is "Homo sapiens", indicating that it belongs to the genus Homo.

Scientific nomenclature of species is important because it universalizes the way to refer to a species making it easier for people of different languages and cultures to understand each other. Same species that have very different names in different regions of the planet can be identified easily by their scientific binomial name which is universally accepted.

Some of the basic rules are:

- Scientific names should be used in place of local or regional names.
- No two genera should have same generic name.
- Zoological nomenclature is independent of botanical nomenclature.
- The generic names used in botany should not be used in zoology.
- The names of species are binomial and those with sub-species are trinomial.
- The genus name should start with capital letter and species with small letter.
- The scientific names should be written in italics or underline them.

Q4. Name the units of classification and give their brief account.

Ans. According to rules of nomenclature, the plant is classified in categories which constitute the unit of classification. The sequence and order of its importance are fixed by rules and are arranged in descending order from units of greatest magnitude to least magnitude namely:

- **Family:** To classify any organism of plant or animal the first step is to grouping together individual organism on the basis of relationship and association among them. This group constitute families. The family name is a plural adjective ending with letter **aceae** for plant and **idae** for animal families for giving generic names. For example, Rosaceae is the family from word Rosa. The family name suggested on the basis of stem name is illegitimate unless according to recommended international code.

- **Genera:** Genera are aggregates of closely related species and genus is a substantive noun in a singular number in this concept. The genus is always written with capital letter and it has one generic name for one kind of plant. A genus consisting of a single species is monotypic e.g. *Leitneria floridana*. If genus contain two or more species it is polytypic.

- **Species:** A group of individual plants and animals that are fundamentally alike as species and this concept is a part of name of individual plant or animal. Species are separated by distinct morphological differences from other closely related forms. The species is a concept not defined in exact terms and is not absolute and inelastic. Names of species is a binary combinations consisting of name of the genus followed by single specific epithet. If a epithet is of two words, they should be unite with hyphen. The symbol forming part of the epithet as proposed by Linnaeus are transcribed e.g. *Pinus*

Many different kinds of species have developed by diverse evolutionary and genetic mechanisms. Many species are sexual but some are asexual. Some have arised from polyploidy, changes in chromosome number and mechanisms which need to be emphasised.

CHAPTER-5

Tools of Taxonomist-I

Introduction

The taxonomy is dependent on other biological sciences because it provides inventory of flora and fauna, schemes of identification and classification of plants and animals. Once the classification is done, there must be some methods to identify taxon. In this unit we will study about ecological and phytosociological aspects of taxonomy using some tools of taxonomy. We will also discuss about conservation of biological resources with wildlife sanctuaries and national parks.

Q1. Discuss briefly the importance of field observation for taxonomic study.

Ans. The field observation is very important for understanding relationship of any group of plants. Ecological study of any field where plant is growing gives the information of development of plant, flowering and fruiting including habitat types, soil types etc. Make a detailed study of characters often lost in dried specimens like colouration of foliage and floral parts, smell, presence or absence of latex, corolla vernation, corolla and anther colour before and after dehiscence. Make a note on viscidity of parts like nectariferous organs, pollinating agencies and time of pollination. Texture of foliage perianth and colour of a matured fruit. The root stock characters also provide vital information. The phytosociological study determine natural variation within and between populations.

Assign the collection number to specimens collected from different colonies within the area.

Q2. What is herbaria and museums?

Ans. A **herbarium** is a collection of carefully preserved, pressed or dried plants stored in special cabinets in a climate-controlled room. Herbarium is also the name for the building or facility in which the collection is stored. Many natural history museums, universities, and natural history surveys have herbaria.

Museums are permanent repositories and are source of information about plants and animals called flora and fauna.

Q3. What is the role of Botanic gardens?

Or

Write a note on Botanical gardens.   [June-2019, Q.No.-2 (b) (iv)]

Ans. The botanical gardens makes us to simply enjoy the beauty and variety of nature. In botanical gardens we appreciate the beauty of foliage and flowers. The role of botanic garden are:

- Plants of interest are cultivated and maintained on scientific basis.

- The vegetation of the world is shown on geographical characteristics i.e. Himalayan flora, Alpine flora
- The plants in danger of extinct should be maintained and their species should be saved
- The plant germ plasm collection should be done.
- Research centers should maintained in various fields
- Taxonomic studies should be done on preserved and live plants
- Educational programmes and research should be promote in experimental botany and ornamental horticulture
- Exchange of materials--live, dried and "Index Semidium" i.e. List of seeds offered for exchange.

Q4. Explain what do you understand by "Checks to Increase" as put forth by Charles Darwin.

Ans. It is observed that vagaries in climate always resulted fluctuations in population. The animal move to another area when scarcity of food to area where it is plentiful. Animals also succumb to other animal predators and fall ill, starve and ultimately die. Though 'Death is a way of life' but Darwin suggests"checks to increase' by keeping the number down both by removing animals from the population and by ensuring that few animals survive beyond their reproductive prime. Prevention is essentially birth control while removal of surplus animals means killing them. In captivity most of the checks to population growth are removed.

Q5. What do you mean by type specimen?

Or

Explain Type specimens.   **[June-2019, Q.No.-2 (a)]**

Ans. The specimens on which the species are based are called type specimen. It is the nucleus of taxon and foundation of its name. Once designated the type cannot be changed. **Type specimen** can also be called 'holotypes'. If all the original specimens and even their duplicates called 'isotypes' are lost or destroyed by fire or some other accident, a fresh specimen can be collected and name them 'neotypes'.

Their value types are given special care by curators of herbaria. Curators of many herbaria do not permit their being sent out on loan to other botanists or institutions.

Q6. Explain the History of Zoological parks.

Ans. Zoo, also called zoological garden or zoological park, place where wild animals and, in some instances, domesticated animals are exhibited in captivity. In such an establishment, animals can generally be given more intensive care than is possible in nature reserves or sanctuaries. Most long-established zoos exhibit general collections of animals, but some formed more recently specialize in particular groups—e.g., primates, big cats, tropical birds, or waterfowl. Marine invertebrates, fishes, and marine mammals are often kept in separate establishments known as aquariums. The word *zoo* was first used in the late 19th century as a popular abbreviation for the zoological gardens in London.

It is not known when the earliest zoos were established, but it is possible that they were associated with the first attempts at animal domestication. Pigeons were kept in captivity as early as 4500 BCE in what is now Iraq, and 2,000 years later elephants were semidomesticated in India. Antelopes, including the addax, ibex, oryx, and gazelle, are depicted wearing collars on Egyptian tomb pictures at ⊚aqqārah, dating from 2500 BCE. In China the empress Tanki, who probably lived about 1150 BCE, built a great marble "house of deer," and Wen Wang, who apparently reigned just before 1000 BCE, established a zoo of 1,500 acres in extent, which he named the Ling-Yu, or Garden of Intelligence.

The biblical king Solomon, who also reigned about 1000 BCE, was a farmer-zoologist, and he was followed, for at least the next 600 years, by other royal zookeepers, including Semiramis and Ashurbanipal of Assyria and King Nebuchadrezzar of Babylonia.

Collections of captive animals were in existence in Greece by the 7th century BCE, and by the 4th century BCE it is probable that such collections existed in most, if not all, of the Greek city-states. Aristotle (384–322 BCE) was obviously well acquainted with zoos; his most famous pupil, Alexander the Great, sent back to Greece many animals that were caught on his military expeditions.

The earlier Egyptian and Asian zoos were kept mainly as public spectacles and only secondarily for study, but the Greeks of Aristotle's time were more concerned with study and experiment. The Romans had two types of animal collections: those destined for the arena and those kept as private zoos and aviaries.

With the end of the Roman Empire, zoos went into a decline, but animal collections were maintained by the emperor Charlemagne in the 8th century CE and by Henry I in the 12th century. In Europe Philip VI had a menagerie in the Louvre, Paris, in 1333, and many members of the house of Bourbon kept collections of animals at Versailles.

In the New World, Hernán Cortés discovered a magnificent zoo in Mexico in 1519. The collection, which included birds of prey, mammals, and reptiles, was so large that it needed a staff of 300 keepers.

Modern zookeeping may be said to have started in 1752 with the founding of the Imperial Menagerie at the Schönbrunn Palace in Vienna. This menagerie, which still flourishes, was opened to the general public in 1779. In 1775 a zoo was founded in a Royal Park in Madrid, and 18 years later the zoological collection of the Jardin des Plantes, Paris, was begun. The Zoological Society of London established its collection in Regent's Park in 1828, two years after the society itself was founded.

By the mid-19th century, zoos were being opened all over the world; among those existing today, more than 40, most of which are in Europe, are more than 100 years old. Since the end of World War II there has been a rapid and worldwide proliferation of zoos, many of which have as their aim not the study of animals but public entertainment and commercial gain. The total number of animal collections open to the public in the world today is not accurately known but exceeds 1,000.

Function and Purpose: The primary object of zoos that are in the charge of scientific societies is the study of animals. Thus, the purpose of the Zoological Society of London, as stated in its Royal Charter, is "the advancement of Zoology and Animal Physiology and the introduction of new and curious subjects of the Animal Kingdom." This society has been the model for many other zoological societies throughout the world. In the 19th century the emphasis of the investigations carried out in scientific zoos was mainly on taxonomy, comparative anatomy, and pathology. Today the opportunities for scientific inquiry are much wider, and a few societies have established special research institutions. In the United States the Penrose Research Laboratory, of the Philadelphia Zoo, is particularly concerned with comparative pathology. The New York Zoological Society maintains an Institute for Research in Animal Behavior and, in Trinidad, the William Beebe Tropical Research Station. In Great Britain the Zoological Society of London maintains, in addition to a modern hospital and pathology laboratories, two general research institutes—the Nuffield Institute of Comparative Medicine and the Wellcome Institute of Comparative Physiology.

Many zoos publish scientific journals and periodicals, which range in their contents from the popular to the highly technical. Again, the Zoological Society of London led the way. Its "Proceedings," now known as the *Journal of Zoology,* has appeared uninterruptedly since 1830.

In recent years a few zoos have intensified their efforts, frequently in cooperation with educational authorities, to provide an educational program for school children and students. Some zoos have full-time or voluntary guides on their staff, whose job it is to provide more information for visitors than can be given on labels attached to cages. Others meet this need by providing "talking labels," prerecorded tapes operated by the visitors themselves.

Since World War II a number of zoos have been developed as breeding centres for animal species in danger of becoming extinct in the wild. Many threatened species have been saved by breeding in captivity. For example, in 1947 it was estimated that there were only

50 nenes, or Hawaiian geese, left on Hawaii and none anywhere else in the world. In 1950 two nenes were housed at the Wildfowl Trust at Slimbridge, England, and in 1951 a gander was hatched. The birds continued to breed successfully, and gradually the captive stock in Europe was spread over a dozen different menageries to minimize the risk of losses from disease or predators. Another species that has been saved by breeding in zoos is the European bison, or wisent, the last wild specimen of which died in 1925. Other species that zoos have helped to survive include Père David's deer and many rare game birds. The increasing number of zoo births gives hope that zoos, rather than capturing wild animals for exhibition, will perhaps be able to restock the wild with zoo-born animals.

WE'D LOVE IT IF YOU'D LIKE US!

We're now on Facebook!

Like our page to stay on top of the useful, greatest headlines & exciting rewards.

Our other awesome Social Handles:

gphbooks
For awesome &
informative videos
for IGNOU students

9350849407
Order now
through WhatsApp

gphbooks
We are
in pictures

gphbook
Words you get
empowered by

CHAPTER-6

TOOLS OF TAXONOMIST-II

INTRODUCTION

In this chapter we will discuss about the taxonomic information collected from morphology, embryology, anatomy, physiology, ecology and other disciplines of biology. Besides this we also learn about documentation of available taxonomic literature, key to identification of plants and animals and about herbarium ethics.

Q1. Give brief account of various evidence required to study taxonomic characters.

Or

Why morphological evidence is essential in systematic research?

Ans. As we know that a systematic approach is necessary for identification of plants and animals, various types of evidences are required for classification. The various types of evidence used as tools are:

- **Morphological Evidence**: Morphological evidence is very important as it is a structure and form of plants and animals which provide the basic language for plant characterisation, identification, classification and relationship. Morphological data are easily observable and obtainable and therefore it is used in taxonomic studies. The growth habit of herbaceous or woody plants is useful in classification. Root system in plants and vegetative underground structure, arrangement of leaves and their venation are some of the characteristics help in classifying plants into dicots and monocots. Natural selection associated with successful reproduction maintains a basic similarity of the reproductive feature of flowers, frujits and seeds within various species, genera and families.

  The families should include mature fruits to insure identification as flower type and fruit are important in classification. The flowers are mostly actinomorphic, perigynous or epigynous and fruits are fleshy pome. The carollas and stamens of figworts provide much information for classification.

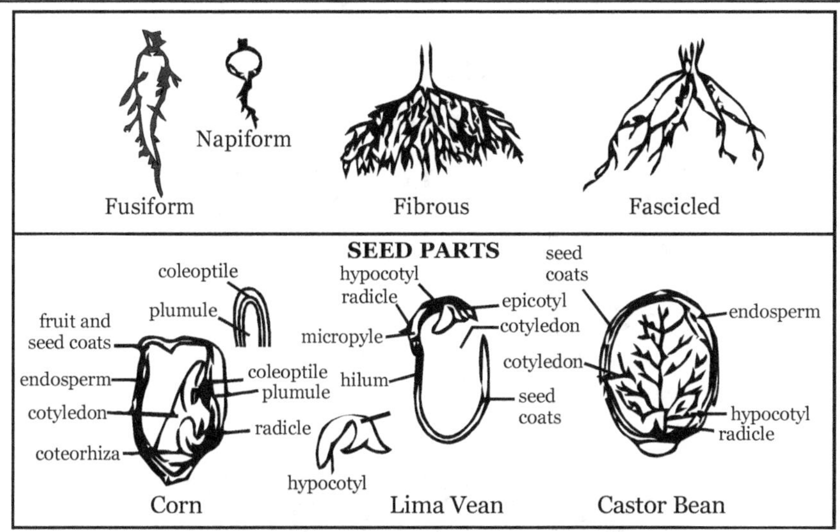

Fig. 6.1

- **Anatomical Evidence**: Anatomy is the study of structure, organisation and development of cells and tissues of plants and animals. The anatomical features of stems and roots are important in separating gymnosperms and angiosperms and also monocots from dicots. The structure of trichomes and their distribution and variation pattern provides characters for classification.

  In animals anatomical structures provide information on characters on which classification is based. The first step is to collect data beyond traditional forms of museum specimens in mammals to the baculeum, to the ear ossicles and to soft parts and second step is to push anatomical observation to deeper levels to cytology and especially Karyology.

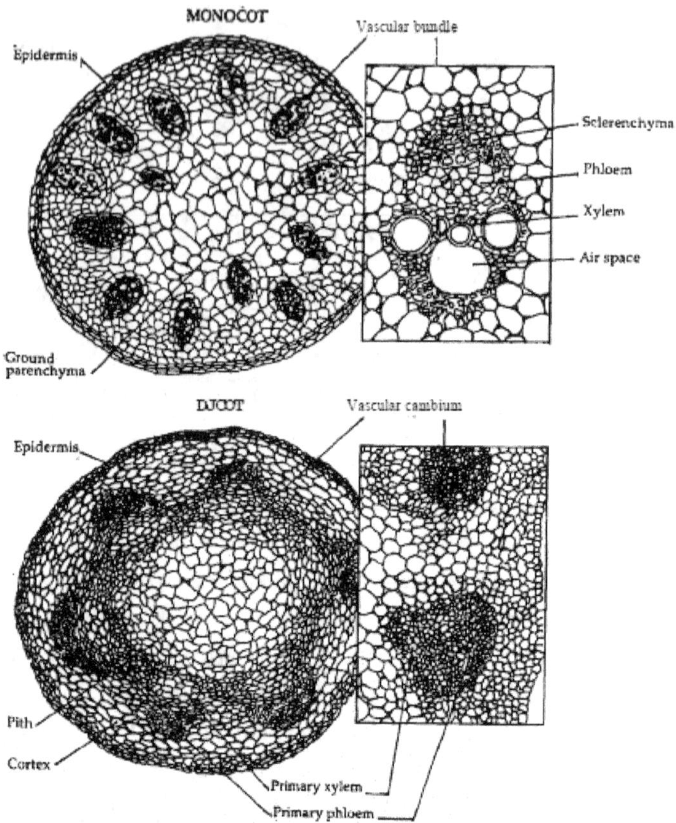

Fig. 6.2

- **Palynological Evidence**: Study of pollen and spores is called palynology. The taxonomic characters of pollen grains include wall structure, polarity, symmetry, shape and grain size. The pollen grains of angiosperms are of two kinds i.e. Monocolpate and tricolpate. Monocolpate pollen grains are boat shaped and have long germinal furrow and apperture and are characteristics of primitive dicotyledons and monocotyledons. The tricolpate grains are globose, symmetrical and have three germinal appertures and are characteristics of dicotyledons.

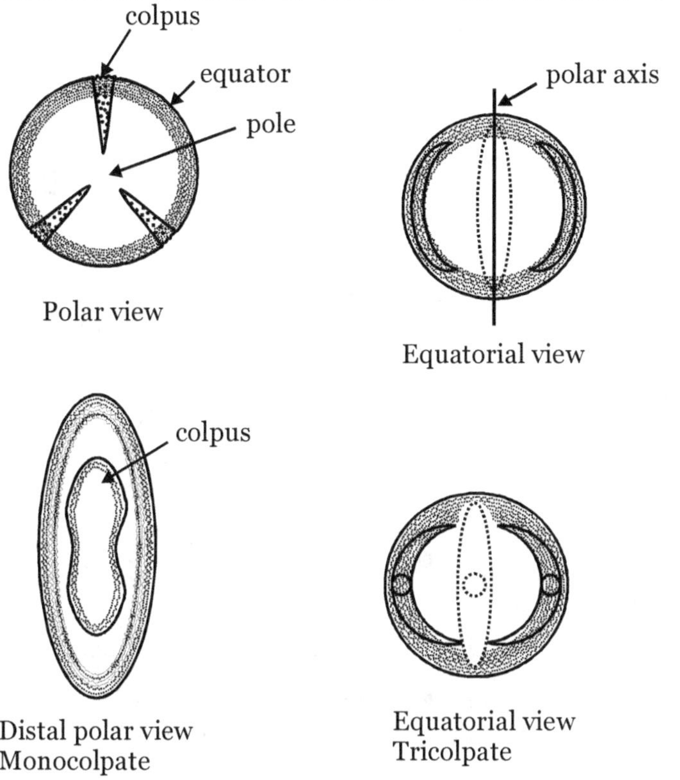

Fig. 6.3

- **Embryological Evidence:** The successive stages of sporogenesis, gametogenesis and the growth and development of the embryo is studied under embryology. The are two or three number of nuclei in the pollen grains at the time of dispersal. In angiosperm double fertilisation is the example of embryological unity. Embryology has systematic significance in the grass family.

In animals the embryological significance is seen in *Anopheles maculipennis* complex is broken into number of sibling on the basis of their egg structure. In fruit flies, the whole eggs are separated on the basis of character of anterior pole and classification of white flies and also based on the structure of their pupae as seen in the figure below.

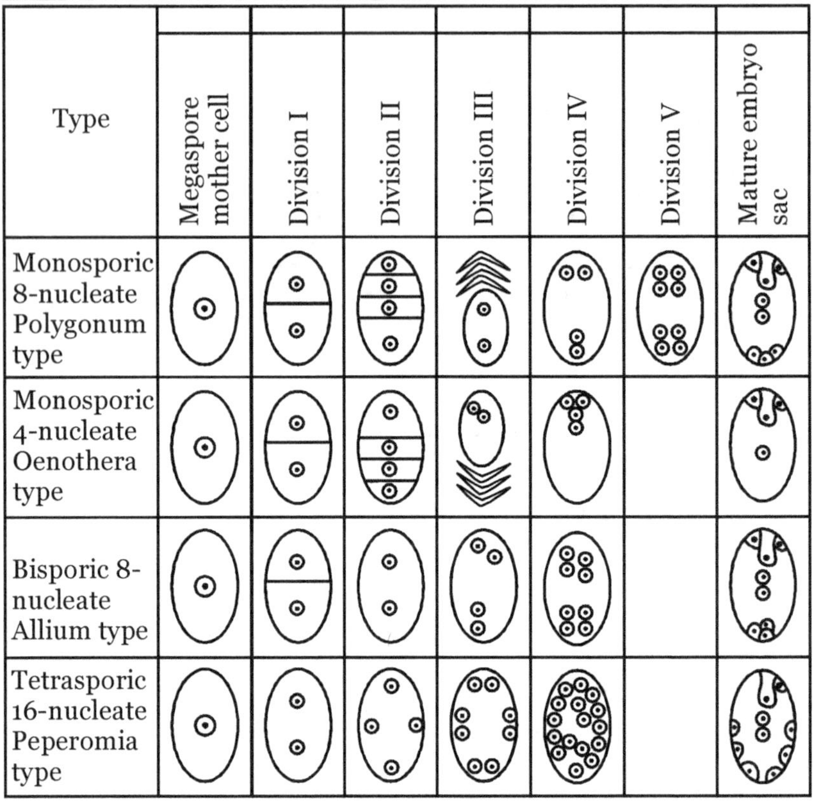

Type	Megaspore mother cell	Division I	Division II	Division III	Division IV	Division V	Mature embryo sac
Monosporic 8-nucleate Polygonum type							
Monosporic 4-nucleate Oenothera type							
Bisporic 8-nucleate Allium type							
Tetrasporic 16-nucleate Peperomia type							

Fig. 6.4

- **Cytological Evidence:** The morphology and physiology of cells are studied under cytology. It gives the information about chromosome number, shape and pairing and behaviour at meiosis which is used for the classification. In angiosperm haploid number of chromosome ranges from n=2 in *Haplopapus gracilis* and n=132 in *Poa littoroea* and most of the angiosperm has chromosome number between n=7 and n=12. About 30-40% of flowering plants are polyploids having higher number of chromosomes because of their multiplication. Flowering plants have several kinds of polyploid number relationship. Pinus is homoploid with n=12, compositae family species have different polyploid numbers like n=90, 18 and 27. There are generawith numbers which show no simple numerical relationship with others called aneuploids for example Brassica with n=6,7,8,9,10. The base number and chromosome size is useful to understand grass family as relatedness of taxa is reflected in homology of the chromosomes, pairing at meiosis in hybrids of two species.

In animals more reliable karyotypes of about 1000 species of mammals, birds and insects are available now for example 16 species of Drosophila are differentiated on the basis of number and shape of chromosomes.

- **Paleobotanical Evidence:** The study of fossils of plant and animals are dealt under paleobotany. The study of microfossils of pollen, leaves, stem are source of information collected from well preserved angiosperm flowers from Eocene sediments of southern United States and diversified representatives from kamsas. Amentiferae line by middle eocene time and their adaptation for wind pollination, flowers and infloresence with structural features allowing pollination by beetles, flies, beas and butterflies. A degree of correlation between chemical compounds of the fossils and those of modern species was found but data available is limited for constructing phylogenetic scheme.

- **Physiological Evidence:** Physiological evidence is very important for plant systematics and recently it has found that anatomical and physiological features are related to carbon fixation in plants and this syndrome is known as Kranz syndrome or C_4 photosynthesis. In algae, mosses, ferns, gymnosperms and many families of flowering plants C_3 photosynthesis is the known carbon fixation cycle. C_4 photosynthesis occurs in 10 unrelated monocots and dicots families. In dicots genus *Euphorbia* C_3, C_4 and CAM (Crassulaceae Acid Metabolism) species are known. In Zygophyllaceae and Chenopodiaceae both C_3 and C_4 carboxylation occurs.

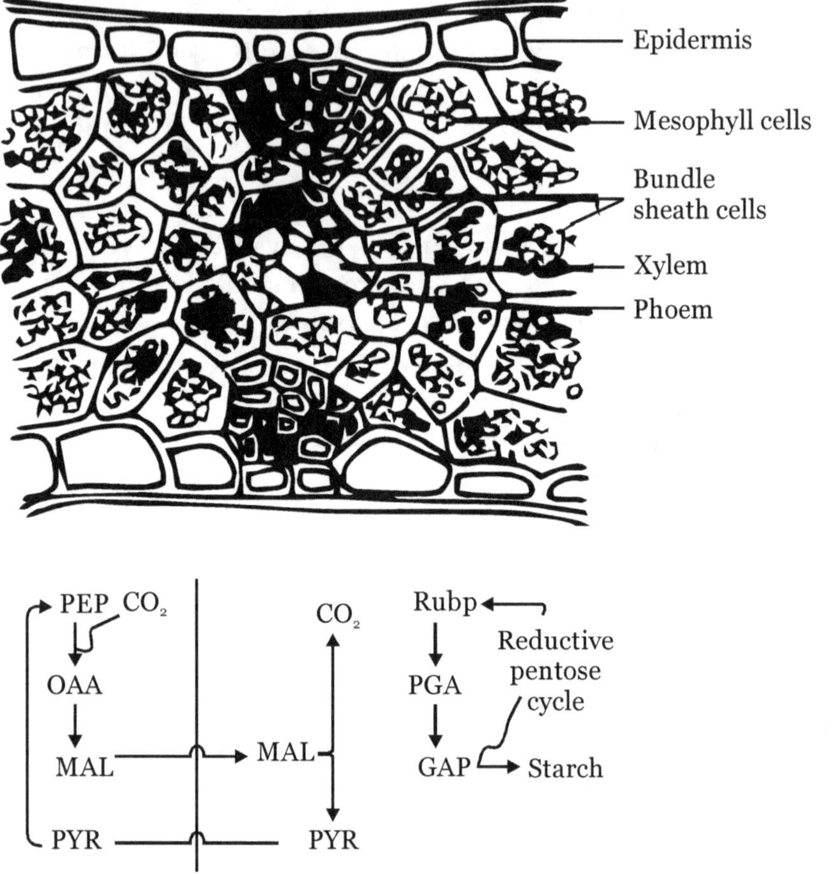

Fig. 6.5

- **Ecological Evidence:** Ecological study depends on morphological features which are correlated with environmental factors like: light, moisture, temperature and fertility. The distribution of taxa of both plants and animals depends on the variation within taxa and adaptations of organism which provide information regarding systematic position of plant and animal species. Ecologist should examine ecotypic variation, edaphic specialisation, pollination, effect of habitat on hybridisation, plant herbivore interactions, seed dispersal mechanism and ecology of seedling establishment. In plants ecological information has implications for classifying it below genus level.

In animals every nearest related species has its preference of food, breeding season, tolerance to various physical factors etc. The two known closely related species coexist in the same habitat avoid fatal competition with their species-specific niche characteristics. The larvae of *Drosophila mulleri* and *Drosophila aldrichi* live simultaneously in the decaying pulp of the fruits of the cactus (*Opuntia lindheimerii*) yet both have preferences for certain yeasts and bacteria.

Q2. What are keys and there types explain in brief? Why is the use of 'key' for identifying a specimen considered more efficient?

Or

What is a key? How are keys prepared and what useful purpose do they serve for a taxonomist?   **[June-2019, Q.No.-3 (a)]**

Ans. Keys are artificial analytical devices used to identify plants and animals based on successive choice between two contrasting characters. Whenever choice is made, one or more taxa are eliminated. In plants keys are part of floras or monographs given before the description of taxa and comprise of statements in a couplet which refer or lead to primary and than to secondary characters. Keys are mainly of two types i.e. Artificial and Natural keys.

(1) Artificial keys: This key is based on resemblances and differences of some prominent characters in taxa. Artificial keys are of two types i.e. Bracketed keys and Indented keys.

   (i) Bracketed Key: It is also called as **Parallel key** because the two leads of the couplet are always next to each other in consecutive lines on the the page. In this at the end of each line there is either name or number referring the couplet later in the key.

       The format in lead can be numbered in alphabets like: A and AA for 1 and 1 and 1' or 1' 1b or B and BB for 22' or 2a2b and number of alphabets are restricted to 26.

(ii) Indented Key: It is also called as Yoked key because collateral leads of a couplet are arranged in yokes and is identify by a number of letters. It is widely used in flora and manuals because each successive couplets is indented a fixed distance from the margin of page for example eight genera of Gentianaceae from geographical region and format like: 1a, 2a2b, 3a3b,1b, 4b4c, 5b5c

(2) Natural keys: This key is based on the phylogenetic relationship between various taxa.

Q3.   How to construct, prepare and use the key for identification?

Ans.   The contrasting characters are used to construct the keys where possible names in the key are divided into smaller to smaller groups. Each time when choice is made one or more taxa is eliminated. Statements in the keys are based on characters of plants like herbaceous vs woody when herbaceous eliminate woody, zygomorphic vs actinomorphic flowers then zygomorphic eliminate actinomorphic flowers and so on. Keys are constructed in a different manner while based on the same matter. A good key is dichotomous and not having more than two alternatives at any point.

The key is prepared by making a choice of characters, considering significant and insignificant characters, tabulating and forming dichotomies of characters. After listing permanent morphological characters, write them in the same sequence on cards and keep one card for each taxon for example if we choose petiole as a character, we have to write it at the same number in all cards but if petiole is absent in plant we have to record it as shown in the table below:

Table 6.1

Characters	Taxa I	Taxa II	Taxa III	Taxa IV
Embryo: No. of Cotyledons	2	2	2	1
Leaves Venation	reticulate	reticulate	reticulate	parallel

Leaves Venation	reticulate	reticulate	reticulate	parallel
Flowers no. of floral leaves	tetramerous	Pentamerous	Pentamerous	Trimerous
Flowers with Perianth	Sepals and Petals	Sepals and Petals	Only one Type	Only one Type
Flowers with Petals	Free	Connate	Usually Absent	Perianth

The first key is used to determine family and next key provide the generic name. After this keying process is repeated within the genus for determination of the species.

If a number of plants ABCDEFG are to be identify, we have to place them in two groups viz. Dicots and Monocots with the aid of keys already there. Following characters are studied for grouping-leaves and their venation, flower- number of floral parts, embryos-number of cotyledons.

Suppose in case of plant ACEF IS provided for recording, the answer to given three characters in the key is identical to those mentioned in the lead, these belongs to dicots, the leaves having reticulate venation, flowers are pentamerous or tetramerous, number of cotyledons are 2 while in plant BD and G charactetrs are identical to those mentioned in lead i.e. Leaves have parallel venation, flowers are trimerous and em,bryo having 1 cotyledon and these belong to monocot.

Following points should be consider while using key:

- Must understand proper terms before use
- Both leads of a couplet be read carefully. When answer to one lead is positive and alternative is negative then we are correct and if answer in both the cases is negative or positive, than there is some mistake.
- If the alternatives in the couplets are not clear and contrasting but overlap then conclusion must be made after checking the description matching with identified species.

- While checking the measurements of organs mentioned in the key, measure more than one parts preferably in 3 replicates and take average. There is always variation in size in fresh and dried specimens.

Q4. What are punch cards and how they are used?

Ans.　　The cards with holes at numbers corresponding to a character are made open by cutting the perforations upto margin. Each number is alloted to the character for example take taxa I-IV as given in the table above then following statement is prepared as:

- No. of cotyledon-1
- No. of cotyledon-2
- Leaves reticulate veined
- Leaves parallel veined
- Flowers trimerous
- Flowers tetramerous
- Flowers pentamerous
- Flowers with sepals and petals
- Flowers with one type of perianth
- Flowers with one whorl of perianth
- Petals free
- Petals fused/connate

If the character is present, the corresponding holes are cut open upto margin when poker is inserted in a bunch of cards at that number and number that is cut open on account of presence of the character fall down and others don't. Two groups are made on the basis of this character. All cards belonging to taxa I will fall out when characters at number 2, 3, 6, 8, 10, 11 are tried and those belong to taxa IV will fall out when characters at No. 1,4,5 and 9 are attempted. Two groups shown at 1 and 1' of the key 2 are obtained as shown in figure.

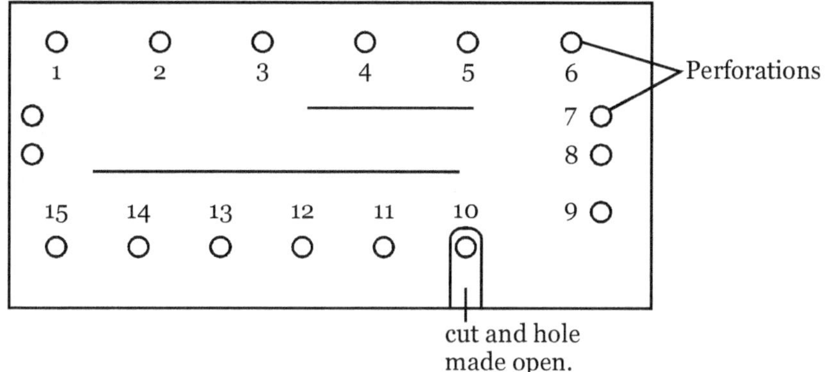

Fig. 6.6

Q5. What do you mean by herbarium and herbarium ethics?

Ans. A **herbarium** (plural: herbaria) – sometimes known by the Anglicized term herbar – is a collection of preserved plant specimens. These specimens may be whole plants or plant parts: these will usually be in a dried form mounted on a sheet but, depending upon the material, may also be kept in alcohol or other preservative. The same term is often used in mycology to describe an equivalent collection of preserved fungi, otherwise known as a fungarium.

The term can also refer to the building where the specimens are stored or to the scientific institute that not only stores but researches these specimens. The specimens in a herbarium are often used as reference material in describing plant taxa; some specimens may be types.

Herbarium Ethics: Always respect and care for the environment from which you are taking flora. No matter where you are collecting, always take only the minimum amount of material required and never collect more than 25% of a single population or more than 10% of the reproductive material.

Endeavour to collect away from the public eye, as others seeing you may not realise that you are collecting in the name of science.

One should strictly adhere to the policy statements. If specimens are dry and fragile, keep sheets flat and mount them on flexible paper. Lift the folder one at a time and avoid placing heavy objects like books, elbows etc. on specimen. Use long armed microscope to study specimen and donot bend the sheet. Donot remove flowers and fruit from the specimen as they are important organs for identification of bspecimen. Inform curator about damaged specimens.

Q6. What are the instruction should be followed while framing the keys?

Ans. Following instructions should be followed while framing key for identification.

- Formation of dichotomies
- Choice of characters
- Significant and insignificant characters
- Tabulation of characters
- Spreading of groups

CHAPTER-7

MODERN TRENDS IN PLANT TAXONOMY

INTRODUCTION

Recent researches have shown that anatomy, palynology and embryology have played a significant role in systematic taxonomy. Cytogenetics and chemotaxonomy have played a great role and have impact on the classification and phylogeny. Exciting developments in the past two decades have been the application of nucleic acid data in systematics has emerged. To understand this a multi-disciplinary approach should be used by taxonomists to analyse data from different aspects of plant biology.

Q1. What do you mean by alpha and omega taxonomy?

Ans. Alpha Taxonomy: It is related to basic classification based on external morphology and empirical approach to classification synthesised from the observed facts. Alpha taxonomy is also called as **Classical or Orthodox or Formal taxonomy.** The Alpha taxonomy word was given by Turril in 1935 while two phase development taxonomy under this approach was studied by Valentine and Love in 1958 and Davis and Heywood in 1963. The two phases are:

- **Exploratory phase:** Involve collection and subsequent classification;
- **Systematic or Consolidation phase:** Involve extensive herbarium collection and field studies for preparing floras, monographs and detailed systems of classification.

Omega Taxonomy: After synthesising the basic classification, taxonomy can be further improved and the observed facts are interpreted in omega taxonomy to provide the interpretive classification. Evolutionary and phylogenetic approaches are used to understand taxonomy of plants at all levels. Omega taxonomy name was given by Turril in 1935. It is also called as **Beta, Neotaxonomy or Modern taxonomy.** According to Valentine and Love in 1958, this represents the biosystematic or experimental phase in the development of taxonomy involving cytological and genetical studies. Davis and Heywood in 1963 suggested that this taxonomy with biosystematic phase also represents encyclopedic or holotaxonomic phase to analyse and synthesises all kinds of information.

Q2. 'Systematic botany is an unending synthesis'. Elaborate.

Ans. There has been a fervour of intellectual activity in botanical systematics during the past 10 years, most of this associated with new approaches to old problems. Constance' has presented an excellent summary of this activity in his account of "Systematic Botany—An Unending Synthesis", and it need only be noted here that he recognizes three major new approaches to present-day systematics, these being:(1) Chemical, (2) Numerical, and (3) Ultrastructural ("Fine Structure").

Keeping in view the statement 'Systematic botany is an unending synthesis' by Constance in 1964, it will be interesting to know about development and understanding of phylogenetic systematics. The term phylogeny was coined by Ernst Haeckel in 1866 which refers to the history of a species and relationship with other species. There is a general agreement as to the definition of systematics and taxonomy.

In view of the current impact of the chemosystematic approach it is perhaps appropriate to evaluate the place of this discipline amongst those of anatomy, cytogenetics, etc. Aiston and Turner have outlined the history of systematics by recognizing five major periods, the inception of each being characterized by the development of new concepts or approaches which have permitted the accumulation of new data and/or conceptual insights bearing on systematics generally. Briefly these are: (1) the Megamorphic (400 B.C.— 1700 AD.), (2) the Micromorphic (1700—1860), (3) the Evolutionary (1860--1900), (4) the Cytogenetical (1900—1960), and (5) the Biochethical (1960--?)t. It should be obvious that each of these periods has made, and continues to make, important contributions to systematics; in fact it might he said that each has contributed in proportion to its time-span. The development of succeeding periods depend upon those preceding, and it is highly likely that any successful evaluation of the biochemical must depend upon the mega- and rnicro-morphical data at all taxonomic levels. That the early 1960s has truly ushered in the Biochemical Era can be ascertained from the fact that four major chemosystematic texts appeared during this period.

Morphological and anatomical characters can be studied by electron microscope to solve taxonomic problems. Plant embryology proved useful as a source of evidence. Cytological and biosystematic data uses information from chromosome number, structure and behaviour useful for taxonomist to study relationship amongst plants.

Chemotaxonomy provides information from chemical characters of plants. Taxonomist can make use of computers to analyse large amount of information in numerical taxonomy and for synthesising classification and the process is continuous one and describe the developments in modern taxonomy to elaborate unending nature of systematic botany.

The brief account on the development in plant classification provided can be concluded with the assumption that 'Systematic botany is an unending synthesis' because every attempt to classify plants into a system of classification has been a synthesis of available information and when new knowledge becomes available, a new attempt shall be made to synthesise a new system of classification.

Q3. (a) Differentiate between " Ranunculaceae *sensu lato*" and "Ranunculaceae *sensu stricto*".

(b) Name the genus which led to above change in the circumscription of the family.

(c) List the important characters responsible for the change.

Ans. (a) This is one of the example of classification of diversity studied by Indian botanist Murgai and Russian Yakovlev and Yoffe. The significant observation was made in embryogeny in Paeonia where genus exhibits a unique embryogeny.

Some of the embryological character differentiate Paeonia from the rest of the family Ranunculaceae as tabulated below. On the basis of detailed information on characters of genus Paeonia was separated from Ranunculaceae and classified as separate family called Paeoniaceae. This difference as a rule of botanical nomenclature differentiate Ranunculaceae into 'Sensu lato' refers to broad concept in taxonomy while 'Sensu stricto' refers to restricted concept after one or more genera have been removed from the family, thus changing the circumscription of the family. So we can say that when genus Paeonia is classified under family Ranunculaceae it is from the family" Ranunculaceae *sensu lato*" and when genus Paeonia is separated from the family Ranunculaceae it is refered as Ranunculaceae *sensu stricto*".

Table 7.1

Feature	Paeonia	Ranunculaceae
Stamen	Spirally arranged, centrifugal	Spirally arranged, centripetal
Anther	Multilayered endothecium, mostly 2-layered tapetum	One-layered endothecium and one-layered tapetum
Pollen	Reticulately pitted exine, large and elongate generative cell	Granular, papillate or smooth exine, small lenticular generative cell
Female archesporium	Multicelled, many megaspore mother cells function	Uni-or multicelled, one cell functions
Antipodal cells	Persistent, not polyploid	Persistent (ephemeral in Adonis), nuclei one or more than one, polyploid
Embryogeny	Unique	Onagrad or, rarely, Solanad type
Seed	Arillate	Non-arillate
Fruit	Follicle	Achene

(b) The Genus Paeonia was first classified in the family Ranunculaceae as broad circumscription but later it was separated from Ranunculaceae giving it restricted circumscription.

(c) There are several aspects which favour the use of embryological characters in taxonomy. The characters are:

- High degree of correlation amongst embryological characters.
- Due to less variability in floral characters, embryological characters show stability.
- Embryological characters are not affected by ecotypic variation and remain unchanged.
- Unlike other angiosperms, the genus exhibits unique embryogeny.

Q4. The common breadwheat , *Triticum aestivum* is a hexaploid. List evidences from the cytotaxonomy and chemotaxonomy to support the evolution of this hexaploid wheat from diploid ancestors.

Ans. The origin of hexaploid breadwheat , *Triticum aestivum* from diploid ancestors has been established cytotaxonomically. *Triticum monococcum* and *Aegilops speltoides* both diploid species can hybridise and the hybrid by chromosome doubling give rise to tetraploid wheat, *Triticum dicoccum*. This can be hybridised with another diploid species, Aegilops squarrosa and by doubling the chromosomes of hybrid, the hexaploid wheat, *Triticum aestivum* is produced.

In chemotaxonomy, protein gel-electrophoresis of seed protein from *Triticum dicoccum, Aegilops squarrosa* and Triticum aestivum provide evidence to show that the hexaploid wheat arose by hybridisation.

Q5. Briefly outline the procedures adopted in numerical taxonomy.

Ans. Numerical taxonomy is an operational science and its procedure is divided into number of repeatable steps.

(1) Choice of Units to be Studied: In numerical taxonomy basic unit is 'Operational taxonomic unit'(OTU). This unit can be used for a single plant when single population of plant is studied to find out the range of variation in plant's characters but if entire plant population is studied as OTU than we are studying single species represented by different populations existing in nature. OTU can be different species with genus is being evaluated. OTU varies with the material studied and this helps the taxonomists in making objective study.

(2) Character selection: After selecting OTU, it is neccessary to select characters by which they are classified and are useful in numerical taxonomy. Many characters are used, preferably minimum of 60 and generally 80 to 100 or more characters are needed to produce a fairly stable and reliable classification. The selected characters have to be coded or given symbol. There are two methods of coding in numerical taxonomy.

(i) **Binary or two-state coding:** This is the simple coding where the characters are divided into + and -, or 1 and 0 but if either of these characters are not present than symbol NC is used indicating for No comparison for the character. This type of coding require more work as large number of variation in plant characters like colour of flower as rose has many colours and if this type of coding is used we have to use each colour as character and will be coded as + or -.

(ii) **Multi-state coding:** This is an alternative method where a single character can be coded in a number of states, each represented by a numerical symbol or code like 1,2,3.....depending on the range of variation. The different colour of roses are given codes like white=1, pink=2 and so on. Besides colour and type of placentation, multistate coding is also useful for quantative characters such as plant height, leaf length, leaf breadth and characters involving measurements. A code is prepared for range of variation and appropriate symbols are alloted to each unit in the range.

After obtaining and scoring the characters the OTU is tabulated as shown in the table below. For example if we have studied 25 OTUs and scored 75 characters from each, the data matrix will contain 25×75= 1875 units of information and to analyse this large number of data, data matrix is essential and can be done with the help of computer.

The information is presented in t×n in table or data matrix consisting of OTUs scored for characters are shown in table below:

Table 7.2

	A	B	C	D
1.	+	+	−	NC
2.	+	+	+	+
3.	+	+	+	−
4.	−	+	NC	NC
5.	+	+	+	+
6.	+	+	−	+
7.	+	+	−	NC
8.	NC	−	+	+
9.	+	+	+	+
10.	+	+	+	−
11.	+	NC	−	NC
12.	+	+	+	−

(3) Measurement of similarity: Overall similarities (s) is calculated by compairing OTU with each other and is expressed in percentage as 100% S for identity and 0% S for no resemblance. A table is constructed between S coefficients for each OTU as shown in fig.:

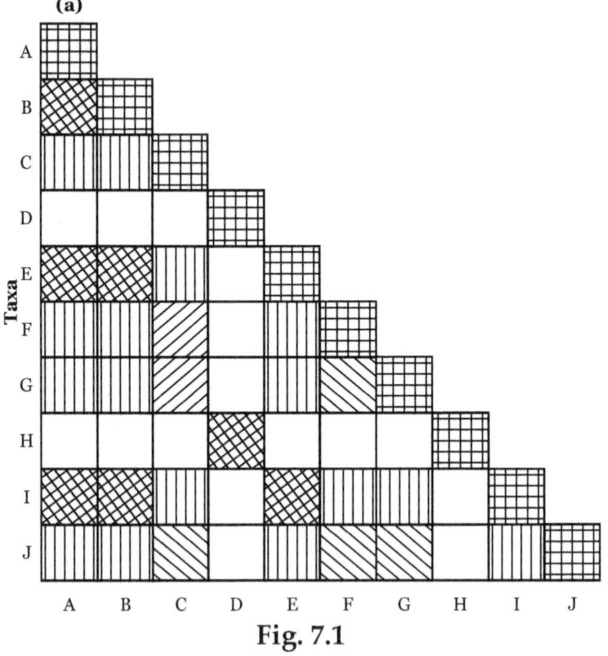

Fig. 7.1

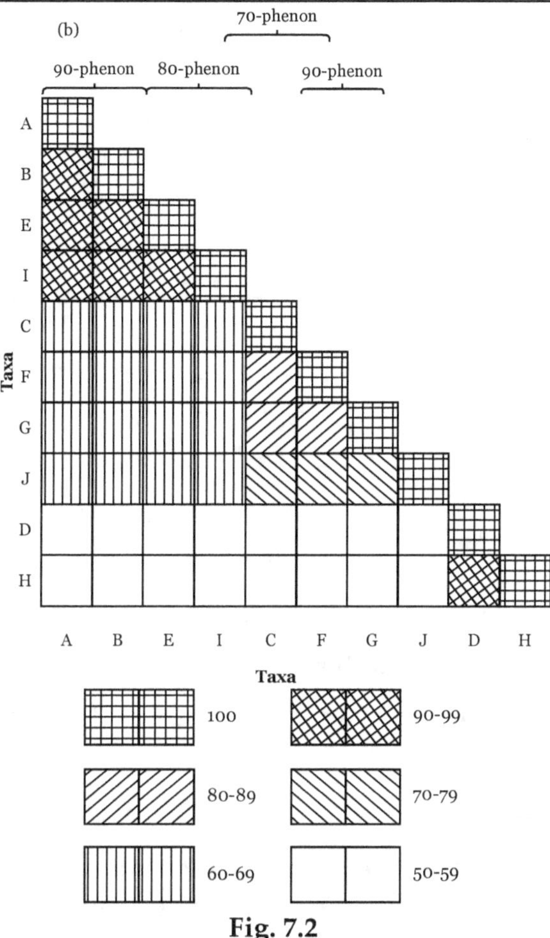

Fig. 7.2

(4) Cluster analysis: The similarity table is rearranged so that OTUs whose members have the highest mutual similarity are brought together. This can be done by different methods and related taxas or groups are recognised. The clusters are called phenons and can be arranged hierarchically in tree diagram or dendogram as shown in the figure below:

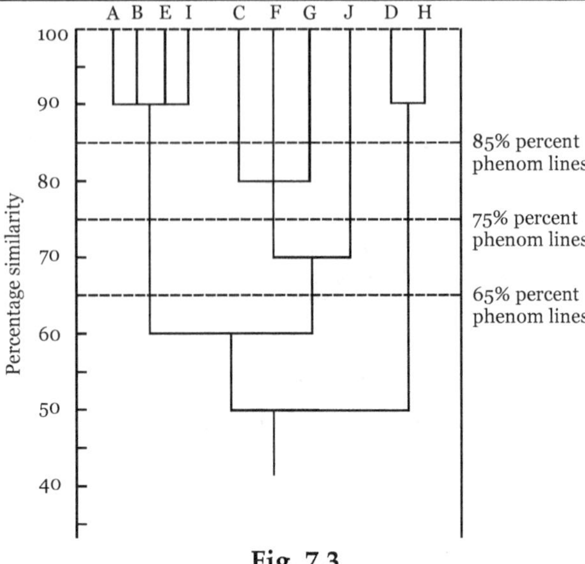

Fig. 7.3

Q6. Write explanatory notes on:

(a) Cytotaxonomy and Biosystematics

(b) Secondary metabolites as characters in chemotaxonomy

(c) Semantides

(d) Chemotaxonomy   **[Dec-2019, Q.No.-6 (d)]**

Ans. (a) Cytotaxonomy and Biosystematics: These are the new approaches adopted in experimental taxonomy to understand variations and is known as **biosystematics.** It is dependent on cytological basis and the cytological data in taxonomy is known as **cytotaxonomy.**

To study this trend in plant taxonomy following points should be considered:

- **Chromosome number:** As we know that number of chromosomes in each cell in single tapecies is constant. Most closely related species are likely to have similar chromosome numbers while more distantly related ones shall have different numbers and this chromosome number is important for taxonomic characters in angiosperms. In the angiosperms from as low as 2n=4 in *Haplopappus gracilis* and as high as 2n=530 in *Poa litterosa*. Large number of angiosperms are studied for chromosome numbers, for example genus Festuca, different species have different chromosome numbers to form mathematical series. The chromosome numbers are 2n=14, 28,42, 56 and 70 etc. And this shows that there is some common basis. If we assume 7 as a common denominator called x and x==7, then we have multiple of this number for different species and x=7 is a basic set of genetic information carried by plant. Such series is said to be polyploid where basic number x is haploid number of chromosomes in a diploid species i.e. X=n=7. The other species are then be tetraploid, hexaploid, octaploid, decaploid etc. Respectively.

- **Chromosome structure:** Chromosome morphology has revealed an interesting feature about chromosome structure is the position of the centromere which provide information about the relationship of 2 arms of chromosome. Depending on the position of the centromere, chromosomes are described as metacentric, acrocentric and telocentric as shown in the figure below.

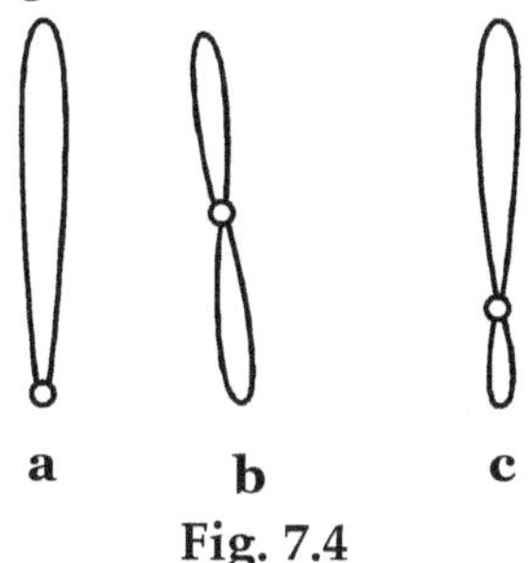

Fig. 7.4

The appearance of the basic chromosome set in a dividing cell is known as karyotype of the cell. This provide information not only on chromosome number but also about chromosome size, volume and type of chromosome in the cell. This information is used by taxonomist for identifying plants and their relationships with species. The karyotype can be represented as an ideogram or karyogram. The interesting observation is that the absolute size of the karyotype is fairly constant as it is controlled by genotype. Taxonomists have found that monocots generally have larger chromosomes than dicots. The smaller chromosomes are found in hardwood plants in comparison to herbaceous relatives.

- **Chromosome Behaviour:** While studying meiosis, we not only observe regularity of pairing which is important for the fertility of plants and also chromosome to chromosome comparison which provide information on the role of chromosomes in heredity. This helps in determining the nature of genome to find out if it is homozygous or heterozygous. Genome analysis in plants is useful in understanding polyploidy and in establishing the percentage of polyploids. A significant study in the case of common hexaploid bread-wheat, *Triticum aestivum*, the genome is designated as AABBDD with 2n=42 chromosomes. Detailed genome analysis have established that 3 diploid species have contributed to the evolution of hexaploid wheat. The A genome is from diploid *Triticum monococcum* 2n=14, B genome for wild grass, *Aegilops speltiodes* 2n=14 and D for *Aegilops squarrosa* 2n= 14.

  Thus, the value of cytotaxonomic data depends upon the information collected by combination of cytological information and data from other disciplines provide useful tool to taxonomists.

(b) Secondary metabolites as characters in chemotaxonomy: Secondary metabolites or plant products are macromolecules that lack nitrogen and are of restricted occurrence and are more important from primary metabolites. This includes compound such as phenolics, alkaloids, terpenoids and usually not involved in vital functions and are largely storage products or pigments. Phenolic compounds of leaves have been very useful for chemotaxonomy purposes.

Both monocots and dicots have been tried for these compounds which show structural variability and chemical stability besides widespread distribution. About 80 species of plants from Ulmaceae family were investigated for flavonoids. Morphological criteria with flavonoid dichotomy can be used to divide the family Ulmaceae (*sensu lato*) into two distinct families: Ulmaceae (*sensu stricto*) characterised by the presence of flavonoid and Celtaceae characterised by the presence of glucoflavonols. Flavonoid chemistry was studied in many families.

The second group of secondary metabolites commonly examined by chemotaxonomists are terpenes. These compounds can be classified on the basis of their molecular structure into monoterpenes, diterpenes, triterpenes and sesquiterpenes used for taxonomic purpose. For example in the genus *Salvia*, 19 species are identify and classify on the basis of monoterpenes. Terpene composition is useful as the morphological characteristics in the analysis of introgression and hybridisation within the genus. Similarly, tri- and sesquiterpenes are useful in classification of families Cucurbitaceae and Compositae respectively. The other metabolites used are iridoid, alkaloids and ellagitannins.

(c) Semantides: Semantides are information carrying molecules in plants and are of 3 kinds namely deoxyribonucleic acid or DNA (primary semantide), ribonucleic acid or RNA (secondary semantide) and proteins (tertiary semantide) following the sequential transfer of the genetic code. Of these, the proteins are the most favoured molecules for chemotaxonomic purposes. Plant proteins can be studied by electrophoresis or by serological methods and processes have been used for obtaining information about the protein chemistry of different plants.

In the common breadwheat, *Triticum aestivum*, the storage proteins were analysed by.electrophoresis and compared with the storage proteins of the tetraploid wheat, *Triticum dicoccum* and the diploid grass *Aegilops Squarrosa* were also analysed electrophoretically. TGS study confirmed that the hexaploid wheat did contain a sum of the proteins possessed by the diploid species which have contributed to the evolution of the hexaploid wheat. This study supports the observations based on morphology and cytological evidence.

Serological analysis of proteins is based on the immunological reaction shown by mammals when a foreign protein is introduced into the system. This is based on the antibody-antigen reaction, the antibodies being specific to an antigen bringing about coagulation. This information can then be analysed to understand the relationships of the different plants on the basis of the serological evaluation of the plant proteins. Serological study is a useful taxonomic tool at different levels of classification. J. G. Hawkes (1960) and his co-workers studied several tuber-producing species of Solanum to understand the evolution of the cultivated potato *Solanum tuberosum* and determine the species of Solanum which could be established as the ancestors of the common cultivated potato, Similarly, in the family Ranunculaceae, serological studies supported cytological data for the classification of the family into tribes and genera. Fairbrothers (1959) and his co-workers have studied several plant groups serologically particularly the members of grass family. A general conclusion from such studies is that the different amount of serological activity in members of different plant families may be interpreted as a reflection of the evolutionary differences in the primary structure of the proteins due to which serological differences can be recognised between members of different families.

(d) Chemotaxonomy: Chemotaxonomy is a recent development in taxonomy which uses chemical information as a character for taxonomic purpose. Chemical characters have high taxonomic value because they are stable, unambiguous and changeable. They also show chemical relationship among plants like morphological characters. The spice plants are identified by aromatic properties and medicinal plants by their curative value and both properties are based on chemical constituents.

Depending on the purpose of investigation, the chemical information may be used for identification of plants or establishing relationships when two or more possibilities are suggested on the basis of morphological characters. All chemical constituents are valuable for taxonomists but some are more useful than other as directly visible in constituents such as crystals, raphides or starch grains occurring in different plants as chemical characters.

Most chemotaxonomists recognise three broad categories of chemical compounds i.e. Primary metabolites, secondary metabolites and sementides useful for taxonomists.

Q7. Write note on Acrocentric chromosome.

Ans. In an acrocentric chromosome the p arm contains genetic material including repeated sequences such as nucleolar organizing regions, and can be translocated without significant harm, as in a balanced Robertsonian translocation. The domestic horse genome includes one metacentric chromosome that is homologous to two acrocentric chromosomes in the conspecific but undomesticated Przewalski's horse. This may reflect either fixation of a balanced Robertsonian translocation in domestic horses or, conversely, fixation of the fission of one metacentric chromosome into two acrocentric chromosomes in Przewalski's horses. A similar situation exists between the human and great ape genomes; in this case, because more species are extant, it is apparent that the evolutionary sequence is a reduction of two acrocentric chromosomes in the great apes to one metacentric chromosome in humans.

CHAPTER-8

MODERN TRENDS IN ANIMAL TAXONOMY

INTRODUCTION

Taxonomy is the science of grouping organisms into different categories according to their physical characters. This grouping, or classification, should be based on homology i.e. the individuals gathered in the same group must shared characteristics that have been inherited from a common ancestor. Thus, to study the modern trends in taxonomy we must go through the history of classification and how this branch has developed with the development of peoples, instruments and techniques. We must keep in our minds that taxonomy today is a reflection of the past, meanwhile the systems of classification reflect both needs, level of knowledge, philosophical concepts and available technology of each historical period.

Modern biologists accept many of the conclusions of the early evolutionary taxonomists, such as the relationships of the major animal phyla, as determined by the comparative morphology of their embryos.

Q1. What are the different stages involved in taxonomic procedures?

Ans. Taxonomy is concerned with describing and naming the many kinds of organisms that:

(1) Exist today, those that has been (2) extinct for many, even million of years ago and those (3) that one become extinct.

Stages in Taxonomy: There are three stages of taxonomy as:

(1) Alpha Taxonomy: It is the level or stage at which the species are4 characterized and named.

(2) Beta taxonomy: It is the analysis of intra-specific variations and evolutionary studies as speciation.

(3) Gamma Taxonomy: It is the analysis of intra-specific variations and evolutionary studies as speciation.

Q2. What do you mean by neotaxonomy?

Or

Explain Neotaxonomy. [June-2019, Q.No.-2 (a) (i)]

Ans. The aim of neotaxonomy or systematic or biosystematics is not only to describe, identify and arrange organisms in convenient categories but also to understand their evolutionary histories and mechanisms. Earlier approaches were primarily based exclusively on observed or morphological data without considering intraspecific differences. Many of the species are thus known by single or few specimens.

Recently, however, great attention is paid to sub-groupings of the species like populations and subspecies. The old morphological species are now called biological ones, which also includes ecological, ethological genetical and other characters. All these new approaches have contributed greatly in explaining the true structure of the species and their evolutionary position and in modification of the basic system of taxonomy. However most of the new approaches need specific methods. Some of these approaches are still developing and provide much excitement by generating new data and information. You should, however, bear in mind that even today it is the morphological features which are used the most, as they are most easily observed, In addition while going through the new approaches you will realise that data from just one approach may not be sufficient to identify organisms.

Taxonomists try as far as possible to use data from as many approaches as possible for accurate identification. Thus today taxonomy is usually called biosystematics or systematic or evolutionary taxonomy or neotaxonomy as it tends to place organisms which share a common ancestor (monophyletic Bncestory) within the same group. Inference of ancestory is based upon similarity and difference among organisms. These differences and similarities are not limited to morphological traits alone. They include a wide variety of similarities and differences in behaviour, embryological structures, fine morphological details with the help of electron microscopes, biochemistry, ecology, cytogenetical data and statistical data.

Q3. How electron microscope is useful in modern taxonomy?

Ans. The invent of electron microscope has made possible for taxonomists to obtain useful ultrastructure of various morphological characters which was difficult to study with necked eyes or light microscopes. Now a days scanning electron microscope (SEM) is extensively used to study invertebrates, particularly arthropods as these insects have fine features. This microscope has much greater magnification and resolution and gives 300 times more depth of focus, three dimensional images of body surface with magnification of 50 to 10,000 x.

In *Argus* the SEM studies have helped in finding new characters which lead to discovery of new species and also in preparation of dichotomous keys. The use of transmission electron microscope (TEM) show greater magnification than SEM and useful in studying the animals and their eggs and embryos. TEM study has helped in the identification of two related genera of protozoan i.e. *Ameoba* and *Thecameoba* and also biosystematics of the planarians, *turbellaria*. It also helps in the identification of two economically important fruit flies, *Dacus olae* and *Ceratitis capitata* whose eggs show superficial similarity in shape and size and are separated on the basis of character of anterior pole studied by SEM but TEM study show distinct differences in their eggs shells. The book you can most believe–GPH book.

Q4. What are the different approaches used in taxonomy to study animal systematics?

Ans. The trends of taxonomy are not only to identify, describe and arrange animals in convenient groups or categories but to understand their evolutionary history and mechanism of evolution.

Now the taxonomy is made to sub-grouping of species like sub-species and population. The old morphological species are now called biological species which include ecological, genetically and biochemical character. The current taxonomical approaches involve e in explaining the true structure and evolutionary position of the species.

The different modern taxonomical approaches are:

- Morphological approach.
- Immature stages and embryological approach.
- Ecological approach.
- Behavioural approach.
- Cytological approach.
- Biochemical approach.
- Numerical taxonomical approach.
- Differential systematic approach.

We will study some of the approaches where uses of electronic microscopes are very neccessary.

(1) Embryological approach: Animal systematics is not just a study of adult animals but study of embryonic and juvenile stages are equally important for the identification of organism having several distinct larval stages. The study of adult and larvae helps in understanding distinct morphological characters. There are many animal groups where classification is of great help by using the immature stages. The study of egg structure has been used to resolve the *Anopheles maculipennis* complex into a number of sibling species. Embryological studies have helped in the classification and separation of species of those animal groups whose morphological traits are less reliable for example sponges.

(2) Ecological approach: This approach use ecological data in systematics where identification of closely related sibling species occupies its own niche in nature which differs from its closest relative in terms of food preference and breeding tolerence to various physical factors. When two closely related species exist in the same habitat they avoid inter specific competition by differing in their ecological characteristics like food preference.

Ecological data in systematics helps in the identification of several animal species such as *Drosophila mulleri* and *D.aldrichi* both live in same habitat i.e. Decaying pulps of fruits of cactus *Opuntia lindheimeri*. They are separated on the basis of their specific preferences for certain yeasts and bacteria. Similarily, *Anophelese maculipennis* complex has been broken in six species on the basis of ecological differences as seen in table below:

Table 8.1

Species	Water Type	Habitat	Hibernation
Atroparrus	Brackish	Cool water	−
Labranchiae	Brackish	Mostly warm water	−
Maculipennis	Fresh Water	Cool running water	+
Melanoom	Fresh Water	Rice Fields	−
Messeae	Fresh Water	Cool standing water	+
Saccharovl	Often brackish	Shallow standing water	−

(3) Ethological approach: Ethological or behavioural characteristics are useful in identification of closely related species. The ethological characteristics are genetically determined and are transmitted from generation ton generation. They play an important role in isolating mechanism and in initiating new adaptations.

Some important ethological characters used in animal systematics are: a. Sound production; b. Bioluminiscence and c. Various other ethological activities.

(i) Sound production: The sound produced by various animal voices and their mating calls recorded on the spectrogram or sonogram are unique for each species and this uniqueness of mating calls plays an important role in speciation or isolation mechanism. The females of particular species are attracted and respond to the matting or breeding call of their own male species. These spectrograms of mating calls in birds have helped in identifying closely related species.

(ii) Bioluminescence: Some animals exhibit pattern produced by bioluminiscence which is useful in identification of sibling species like fire fly, *Photuris*.

Strain code	Source	Salinity (ppt)	Grams Nature	Luminescence Properties
SQ1a	Squid	-	Gram negative rod	positive
SQ4a	Squid	-	Gram negative rod	positive
PD1	Port Dickson Beach 2°30'7.77"N 101°50'11.01 "E	30.1	Gram negative rod	positive
SP1	Sungai Sepang Besar Jetty 2°36'32.74"N 101°42'11.97 "E	29.8	Gram negative rod	positive
PJ1	Pantai Leka, Parit Jawa 1°56'59.21"N 102°37'59.08"	29.1	Gram negative rod	positive
PJ4	Pantai Leka, Parit Jawa 1°56'59.21"N 102°37'59.08"	29.1	Gram negative rod	positive

Fig. 8.1

The study of the frequency, intensity, colour and shape of individual flashes, flash sequences which may be of short or long duration of constant intensity. It may increase or decrease and make it possible to identify 18 sibling species of *Photuris* instead of three species known earlier. Besides bioluminiscence, other differences have come to light in terms of habitat and breeding season and body colour.

(iii) Other ethological activities: Comparative studies of behaviour or activities are useful in systematics and identification of organisms like fidler crab (*Uca*) show that males display their large right chelipads as characteristic which makes possible to recognise closely related species from a distance.

The nest building and its structure is also used in systematics and useful in identifying birds, insects and some other animals. It is also useful in separating two morphologically similar bees of genera *Anthidium* and *Dianthidium* by type of material used in nest or hives contruction by them. The former uses cotton plant fibers while later uses resinous plant exudations and sand or pebbles.

The other ethological characteristics used in systematics is the nature and type of web construction used for the identification of mites, caterpillars and spiders. So the ethological data is frequently used in systematics along with taxonomic information from other approaches.

Q5. Give an account of cytological approach in taxonomy.

Or

Write note on Karyological study.

Ans. Cytotaxonomy in animals deals with structural, genetical and biochemical aspects between organisms ti identify them. The two types of data commonly used is:

- **DNA hybridisation study:** In this technique deoxyribonucleic acid(DNA) of two organism is extracted to compare the genetic affinity between the two. Then DNA strand of both are separated and single strand come in contact with each other in vitro in order to hybridise them. The degree of hybridisation is an indicator of the closeness or distantness of two organism. The use of this technique in estimating genetic similarities among vertebrates are shown in table below:

Table 8.2

Compared Taxa	Percentage Difference in DNA Sequences
House mouse-Norway rat	20.0
Cow-pig	20.0
Cow-sheep	7.5
Human-chimpanzee	1.6
Human-gibbon	3.5
Human-rhesus monkey	5.5
Human-galago	28.0

DNA matching or hybridisation holds a great promise in solving taxonomic problems.

- **Karyological study**: **Karyotype** is the configuration or number and structure of the chromosomes at metaphase. The data is used in the karyological study in biosystematics.

The configuration or number and structure of the chromosome at metaphase is used in biosystematics of animals either sepatately or together. Chromosome number is cponstant within the species but may vary from one species to another within the same genera. In animals the chromosome number ranges from a diploid of 2 in Parascaris equorum var univalins to 446 in Iycaenid butterfly, Lysandra atlantica. In most animal it is between 12-60 chromosomes.

Chromosome number is not enough for identifying organism.in marsupial family *Didelphidae opossums*, species of genus *Monodelphi*s have diploid 18 chromosomes and of genus Didelphis have a diploid 22 chromosomes. In Trichoptera, the chromosome number has been used to plot phylogenetic relation among various families as shown in figure below:

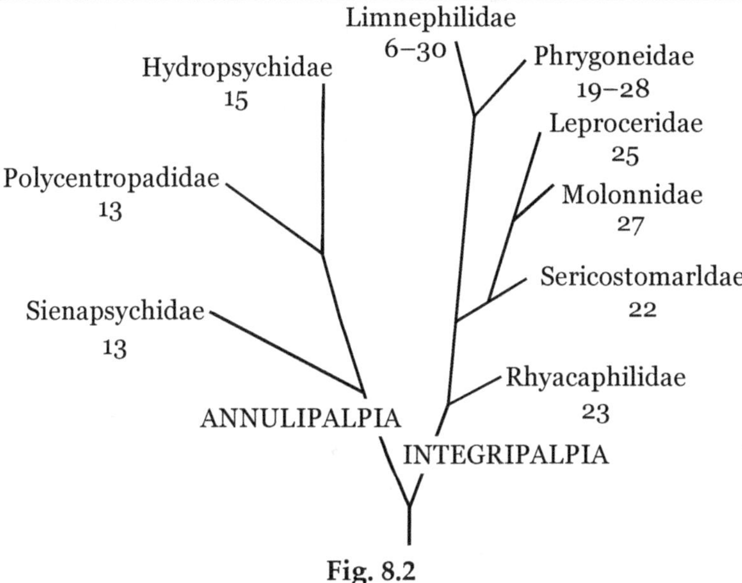

Fig. 8.2

In most cases chromosome number is not enough for identification because different genera may have same number of chromosomes. Hence structure of chromosome is important here because it may vary from organism to organism. In karyotypes we study, the dimensions of each chromosome, position of centromere and presence or absence of secondary constriction.

The differences of centromeric position in the X chromosome of species of genus *Marmosa* has helped in classification. In *M. Robinsoni* it is metacentric, in *M. Murine* it is submetacentric and in *M. Alstoni* it is acrocentric as shown in the figure below.

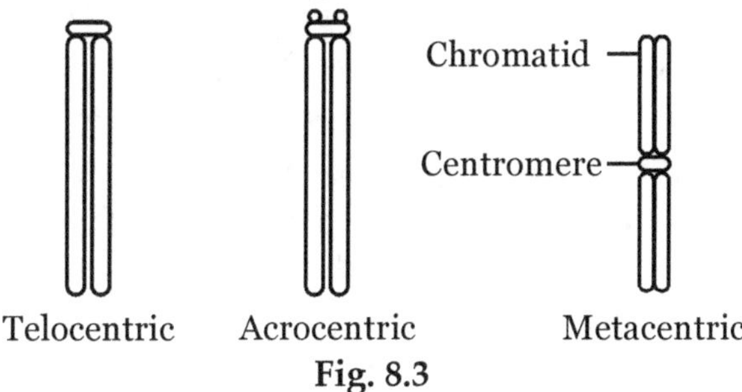

Fig. 8.3

The recent improved technique in cytology is tried on difficult animal groups like birds, mammals and insects resulted in reliable karyotypes like one thousand species of mammals, several hundred species of fishes, amphibians, reptiles and birds. Numbet of species complexes have broken in the case of mammals, urodeles and insects show two synonymised species of earwig, genus Labidura differentiated on the basis of karyotype. So, karyotype in animal systematics help in identification. In grasshoppers, there is great uniformity in the Acrididae (2n= 23 acrocentrics) Pamphagidae (2n= 19 acrocentrics) and Pygomorphidae (2n= 19 acrocentrics).

It has been observed that in some animal groups, the karyotype has remained substantially constant throughout evolutionary stages while in others it has undergone distinct changes, even in closely related species. For example, insects belong to Odonta, Diptera and Coleoptera, the chromosome number has remained fairly constant while in insects of Lepidoptera, Trichoptera and scorpions and fisheshas exhibited marked variations.

Q6. Explain biochemical approach and what are the types of differences found in protein taxonomy?

Ans. In this approach taxonomists study the differences and similarities in the biochemical data for identification, comparing the chemical compounds which perform same function in different animal species. The comparison is done on the basis of biochemical properties and distribution of compound in different organ of the body. Mostly compounds of proteins, amino acids and peptides are studied for the purpose and that is why biochemical taxonomy is referred as 'Protein taxonomy'.

The two main types of differences are found in protein taxonomy.

- **Relative quantitative difference:** Study involves analysis between amounts of different proteins and different constituent of amino acids in proteins of different animals. For example in birds, the phylogenetic relationships among various order has been done on the basis of quantitative analysis of ascorbic acid produced in the kidney of some birds, in some in the liver and in some kidney and liver both and in some neither of two. This analysis show that the ancestral enzyme systems involved occurred first in kidney, later transferred to liver and finally lost in some of the more evolved passerine birds.

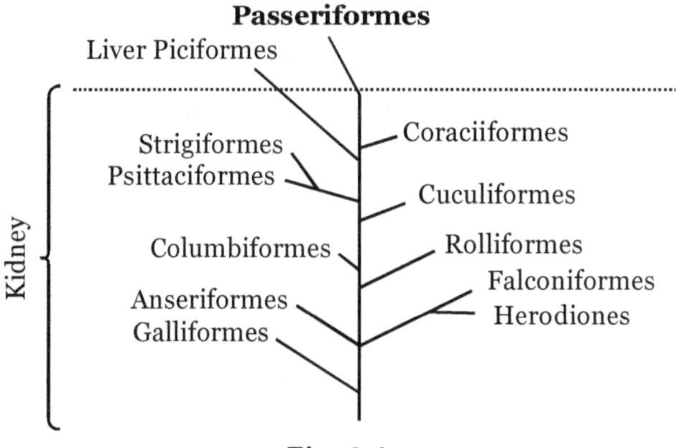

Fig. 8.4

- **Quantitative difference:** Here animals are identified by two types (i) By analysis of amino acid sequence on particular peptide in various animals. (ii) By comparison of particular protein and number of similar amino acid or peptides present in different animals.

The analysis of relative order or sequence in which amino acid is arranged with polypeptide has significance. The structure of fibrinogen from various species provide valuable information in mammalian classification. Amino acid sequence in fibrinopeptide of 34 different mammalian species involves splitting off of fibrinopeptide from the parent fibrinogen molecules by the action of thrombin.

The fibrinogen molecule consists of three polypeptide chain(α, β) linked to disulphide bridges as shown in the figure below.

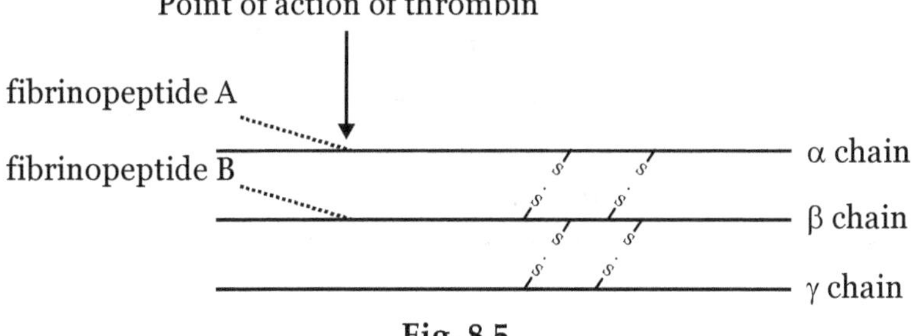

Fig. 8.5

The proteolytic enzyme, thrombin splits off two fibrinopeptides, one from α and one from β chain and are known as A and B fibrionopeptide sequence.

The classification worked out on the basis of amino acid sequence in peptides have been found in agreement with the classification based on morphology. So, it is possible to construct phylogenetic relationship on the basis of amino acid sequence in peptides.

Other peptide in amino acid sequence has proved useful in identification is cytochrome C which is present in the cells of living organisms having 110 amino acids. This fits fairly well with current classification.

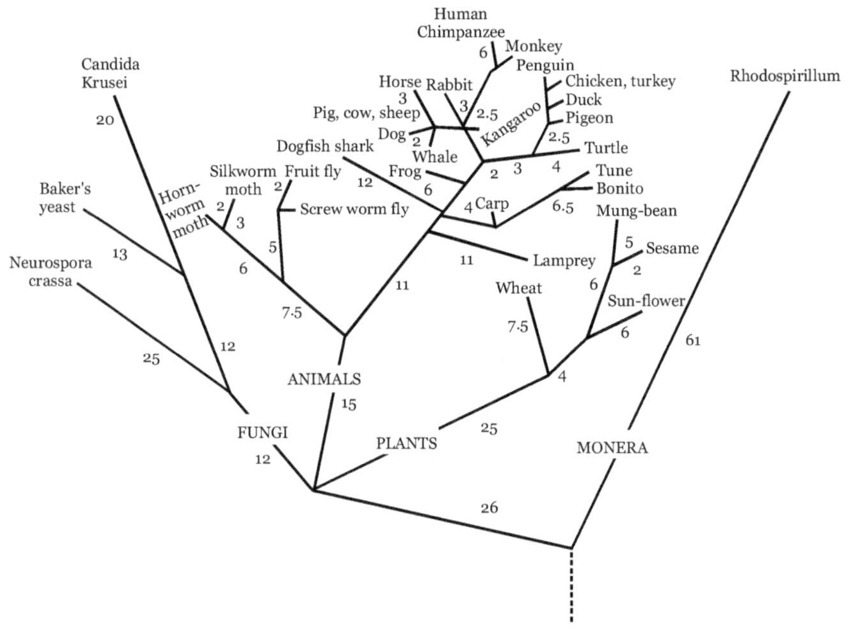

Fig. 8.6

Comparison of particular protein in different animals: To have full sequence analysis of protein in order to discover evolutionary affinities. To do this required chemicals are separated in different species to compare the results. This study reveal similarities and differences in related species. To separate these chemicals certain techniques used are:

- Chromatography

- Electrophoresis
- Immunology study

Q7. Write notes on the following:

(a) Chromatography

(b) Electrophoresis

(c) Immunology study

Ans. (a) Chromatography: This technique is used to identify amino acids in the proteins of organism. To do this the protein is hydrolysed by appropriate enzymes into its constituent amino acid then separated by chromatography. In taxonomy paper chromatography is used to compare the chemical composition of closely related species. The compounds used are peptides and amino acids treated by nonhydrin to reveal the presence of amino acid gives blue liliac colour on heating. The spots obtained are identified by the comparative distance they move in both direction as seen in figure. The spots of amino acid and peptides of each species form a unique pattern called chromatogram.

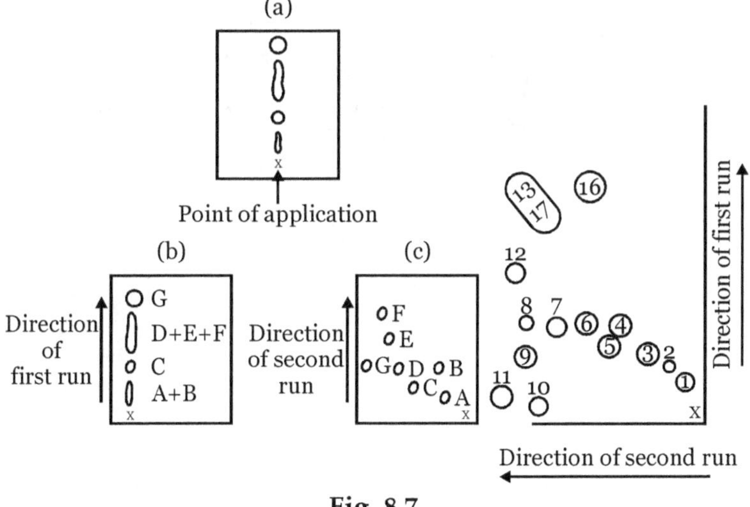

Fig. 8.7

Chromatographic technique have helped in identification of number of anim,al specie. About 21 amino acids have been detected in adult mosquitoes and helped greatly in systematics. Similarly species of lymnae(gastropods) and fishes have been separated on the basis of amino acids occurring in their muscle protein.

(b) Electrophoresis: This technique is similar to chromatography as it involves the similar movement of dissolved organic molecules through a fixed medium but in this case the movement and subsequent separation and identification of the organic molecules is due to the potential difference created by an electric field. Electrophoresis is simply the movement of ions in solution under the influence of electric field. The negatively and positively charged molecules move in opposite direction.

The rate at which ions or charged molecules move depends on their size, shape and other characteristics. Electrophoresis is used to compare protein profiles to determine the relationship between species as seen in the figure below:

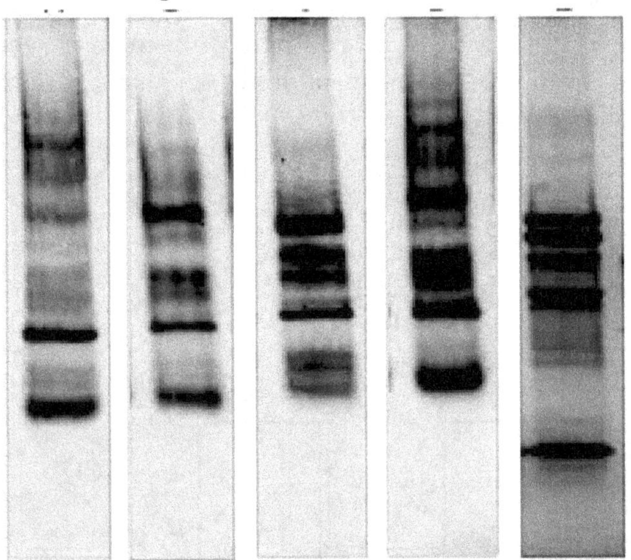

Fig. 8.8

The proteins migrate in response to the electric field, their speed depends on chemical makeup. When exposed to an appropriate agent the proteins can be observed and their pattern can be compared which indicate a close relationship between the organisms. Boundary or moving boundary electrophoresis is now replaced by ' zone electrophoresis' in which the solution containing the ions is supported in materials like paper, agar, starch, acetate cellulose or polyacrylamide.

Disc electrophoresis is most commonly used form of zone electrophoresis but these procedures are unable to separate proteins of similar mobility. The separation of proteins of similar mobility but dissimilar molecular size is done by latest technology called 'polyacrylamide gradient gel electrophoresis'where protein migrate through small pores, the sizes of which is regulated by adjusting the gel concentration. The proteins are retarded and stop when the pore size becomes too small for further movement and this leads to edge of migrating zones, thus giving rise to compact concentrated zones.

In the two directional electrophoresis, first the separation of molecules of similar size along one axis and further separation according to their mobility by running the zone electrophoresis at right angles to the first.

Electrophoresis in systematic study has helped in comparative identification and phylogenetic relationships. Electrophoresis has shown the biochemical difference in amino acids of various animals like oxen, horses and sheep and pigs. For instance, the insulin of the oxen, horses and sheep was found to be different; the ACTH of pig was found to differ from that of oxen.

Electrophoresis of egg white of birds have shown phylogenetic relationship and subsequent construction of hypothetical dendodogram of their relationship. This relationship is seen in flamingo, typical duck, typical heron. The profiles for heron and flamingo remain but gradually diverge from that of duck indicating that heron and flamingo are more closely related than the duck as seen in the figure below.

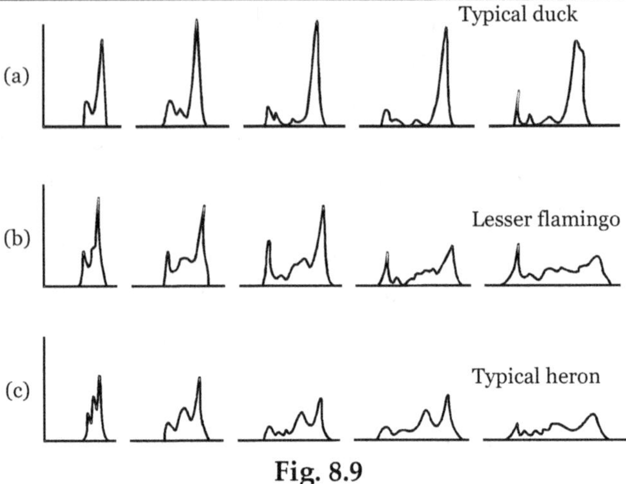

Fig. 8.9

Flamingos have been classified with the help of electrophoretic profiles of Phoenicopteridae (flamingos), Anseriformes(ducks, geese), Ciconiiformes(storks, herons) and Charadriiformes (sand pipers) and a hypothetical dendogram of their relationships has been constructed as seen in the figure below:

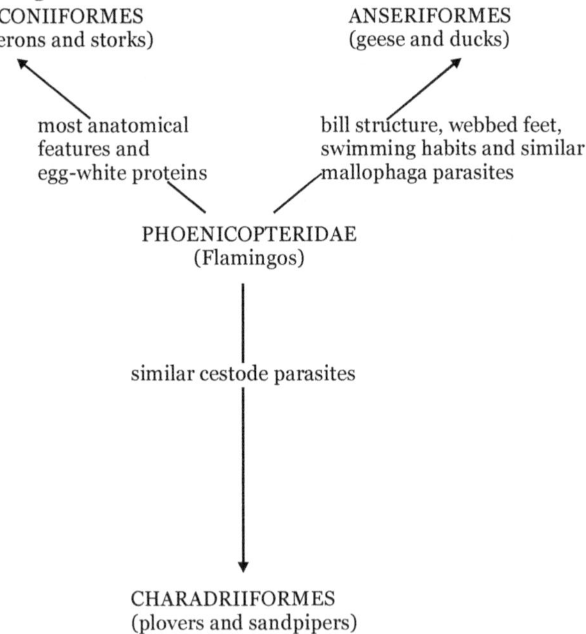

Fig. 8.10

This technique is useful in molluscan taxonomy, to separate some species of genus Bulinus through their egg protein studies. Electrophoresis studies for identification of number of other animals have been carried out by using various substances for analysis. Recently, in addition to the use of enzymes, substances like milk, tears, haemolymph, snake venom, liver and muscles are also analysed for identification.

(c) Immunological study: The study is based on immunological and serological techniques done on organism closely related having similar but not identical genotypes. For example if we want to find out affinity between human and some other animal, if we inject human serum protein into rabbit, the later responds by producing protein and antibodies against the antigens in the serum. If this antibody is mixed with the serum of number of animals separately resulted into a precipitate and the degree of precipitation of antigen-antibody reaction indicates the degree of relationship and is known as 'homologous or 'reference reaction'..

The precipitation is total when it is between antibodies and specific antigen that originally stimulated their formation. When the precipitation occurs but to a lesser extent i.e. the antigen is chemically different but related to original one which stimulated the antibody production is known as ' heterologous' or 'cross a reaction' as shown in the figure. Complete absence of precipitate indicates difference in relationship of organisms.

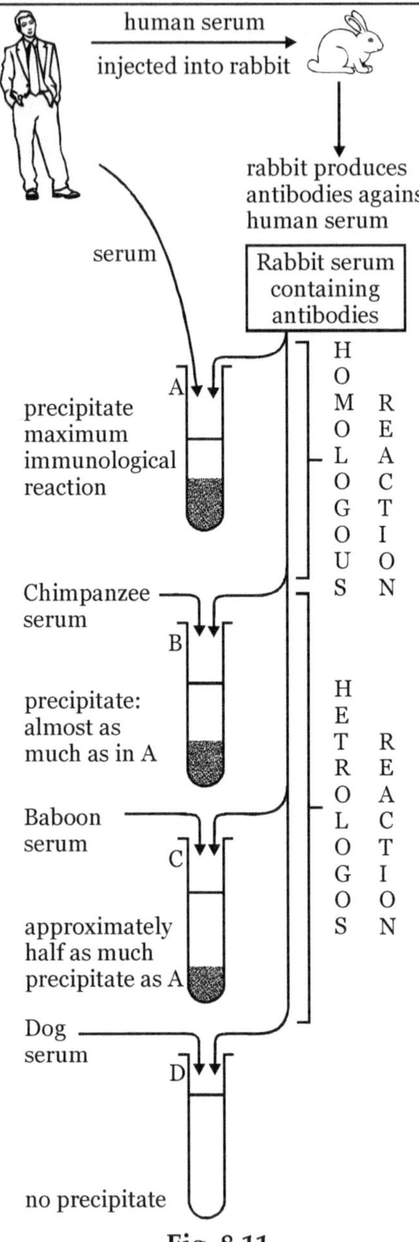

Fig. 8.11

The more closely the related animals, the greater the similarity in the chemical make up and antigen derived from them. In heterologus, the more closer the animal taxonomically anfd produce antibodies, the greater will be the degree of precipitation. This the 'Law of proportionality' and immunotaxonomy or serotaxonomy are based on it. The antigen used for stimulating antibody production may be egg proteins, serum proteins, eyelens proteins, tissue homogenates. The comparative precipitative reaction in immunotaxonomy of animals are studied by following technique:

- Ouchterlony and gel diffusion methods: In gel diffusion techniques, the antigens and the antibody are allowed to diffuse through the gel, mostly agar and a line of precipitation occurs where the meet. In double diffusion method of Ouchterlony, gel is placed in petridish and circular wells are cut in agar and well contains antibody in the centre. The antibody diffuses outwards towards the antigen containing wells and then meet the antigens from same animal, (a) the arcs become continuous, (b). Where there is partial identity an arcs may occur but a peripherally projecting spur, (c) In the case of non identity the arcs do not join but cross one another.

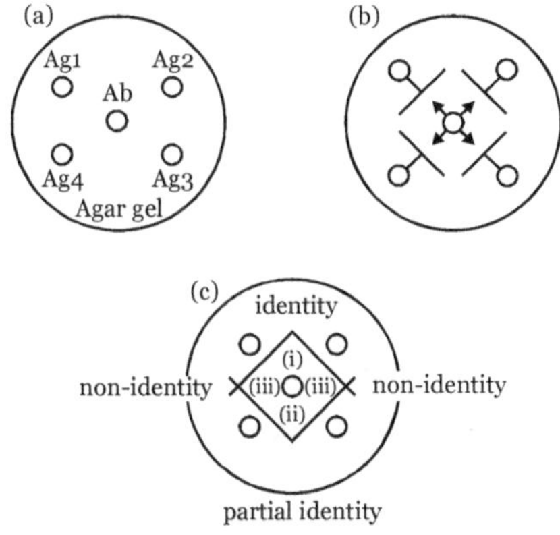

Fig. 8.12

- **Immunoelectrophoresis:** This technique is usedin multiple systems where a mixture of antigen in a single well and corresponding mixture of antibodies are used when it becomes difficult to interpret the arcs correctly. In this method the antigens are separated first on the basis of electrophoretic mobility and then it is allowed to diffuse through gels towards the line of diffusing antibody and precipitation arcs forms where they meet.

This method is carried out on microscale using gel, coating one surface microscope slide of polyacrylamide like starch, agar etc. As seen in figure below:

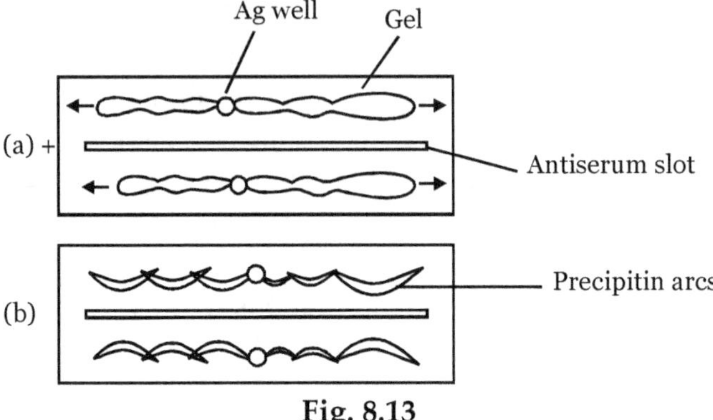

Fig. 8.13

This study helped in animal systematics and determining the interrelationship of species within a group as seen in crab in the diagram below:

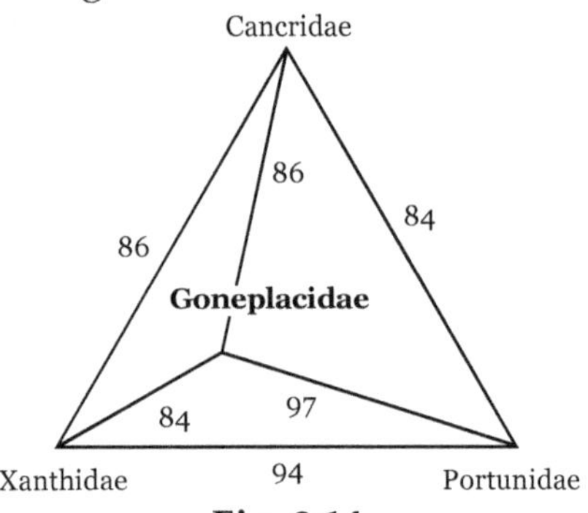

Fig. 8.14

Immunotaxonomy also helped in the confirmation of affinities and phylogenetic analysis and forming of phylogenetic tree of primates, based on immunoelectrophoretic studies of vertebrate eye-lens proteins and also in the discovery of a large number of geographical races and sibling species.

CHAPTER-9

CONCEPT OF ORGANIC EVOLUTION

INTRODUCTION

The present concept of evolution is a modified form of the Darwin's theory of natural selection and often called Neo-Darwinism. According to it only genetic variations (mutations) are inherited and not all varations as held by Darwin. Thus modern concept of evolution is synthesis of Darwin's and Hugo de Vries' theories. This is also called Synthetic Theory of Evolution. Today, the Darwinian concept of natural selection is fully explained in terms of gene frequencies and the changes they undergo from one generation to the next. The variability today is generated continuously in populations by mutations and further enhanced by genetic recombinations. These processes with natural selection bring about changes in gene frequencies in population.

Q1. Critically evaluate the Lamarckian concept of evolution.

Or

"Acquired characters can not be inherited" Explain.

Ans. George Gaylord Simpson in his book *Tempo and Mode in Evolution* (1944) claimed that experiments in heredity have failed to corroborate any Lamarckian process. Simpson noted that neo-Lamarckism "stresses a factor that Lamarck rejected: inheritance of direct effects of the environment" and neo-Lamarckism is more closer to Darwin's pangenesis than Lamarck's views. Simpson wrote "the inheritance of acquired characters, failed to meet the tests of observation and has been almost universally discarded by biologists."

The botanist Conway Zirkle (1946) pointed out that Lamarck did not originate the hypothesis that acquired characters were heritable, therefore it is incorrect to refer to it as Lamarckism:

What Lamarck really did was to accept the hypothesis that acquired characters were heritable, a notion which had been held almost universally for well over two thousand years and which his contemporaries accepted as a matter of course, and to assume that the results of such inheritance were cumulative from generation to generation, thus producing, in time, new species. His individual contribution to biological theory consisted in his application to the problem of the origin of species of the view that acquired characters were inherited and in showing that evolution could be inferred logically from the accepted biological hypotheses. He would doubtless have been greatly astonished to learn that a belief in the inheritance of acquired characters is now labeled "Lamarckian," although he would almost certainly have felt flattered if evolution itself had been so designated.

Peter Medawar (1985) wrote regarding Lamarckism "very few professional biologists believe that anything of the kind occurs — or can occur — but the notion persists for a variety of nonscientific reasons." Medawar stated there is no known mechanism by which an adaption acquired in an individual's lifetime can be imprinted on the genome and Lamarckian inheritance is not valid unless it excludes the possibility of natural selection but this has not been demonstrated in any experiment.

A host of experiments have been designed to test Lamarckianism. All that have been verified have proved negative. On the other hand, tens of thousands of experiments— reported in the journals and carefully checked and rechecked by geneticists throughout the world— have established the correctness of the gene-mutation theory beyond all reasonable doubt... In spite of the rapidly increasing evidence for natural selection, Lamarck has never ceased to have loyal followers.... There is indeed a strong emotional appeal in the thought that every little effort an animal puts forth is somehow transmitted to his progeny.

According to Ernst Mayr (1997) any Lamarckian theory involving the inheritance of acquired characters has been refuted as "DNA does not directly participate in the making of the phenotype and that the phenotype, in turn, does not control the composition of the DNA." Peter J. Bowler has written although many early scientists took Lamarckism seriously, it was discredited by genetics in the early twentieth century. Lamarckian laws of use and disuse in the inhritance of acquired characters are untenable proposition and any structure if repeatedly used cannot result in adaptation.

Acquired characters cannot be inherited: Lamarck said that the inheritance of characters was acquired during the life time of the individual. This principle has been experimentally found incorrect.

Traits acquired during life time of an individual influence only the non-reproductive organs. There is no influence on the DNA of germ cell. Only the germ cells transfer traits from parents to offspring. Non-reproductive organs have no such role. Traits acquired by them die with the death of the individual. These changes occur in the non-reproductive tissues, these cannot be passed into the DNA of the germ cells. Hence acquired characters are not inherited.

Q2. What do you understand by the term struggle for existence?

Ans. In the Origin of Species in 1859, Darwin claimed that there was a continuous 'struggle for existence' in nature, in which only the fittest would survive. He said that a competition among the individual species is a test to the variations in the traits of the organism useful for them ion a given environment are deemed to be adaptation.

The idea of the struggle for existence has been used in multiple disciplines. It became popular in the mid 19th century, through the work of Malthus, Darwin, Wallace, and others. The most popular use of the struggle for existence is in the explanation of the theory of natural selection by Charles Darwin.

Q3. How the biochemical genetics helped in the understanding of the evolutionary process?

Ans. Biochemical Genetics provides an essential link between the sciences of biology chemistry and genetics by offering an interdisciplinary forum for the discussion of new developments. This concept was proposed by Beadle and Tatum on the basis of their work on bread mould, Neurospora crassa and a hypothesis of 'one- gene-one-polypeptide came forward and a theory was generalised on the basis that not all proteins are enzymes. In biochemical genetics it should be possible to compare the structure of proteins and the sequence of amino acids serving the same functions in different organisms to seek evidence for their evolution.

Through this concept, an anatomical and embryological relationships and differences have been exploited to document organic evolution and to construct a phylogenetic trees.

Q4. What do you understand by the term 'Modern synthesis'?

Ans. The synthetic theory was challenged in 1970 by a palaeontologist, S. J. Gould and suggested that the fossil record revealed that evolution had occured in spurts punctuated by long periods of equilibrium or stasis and named the concept' Punctuated equilibrium'. This concept suggested that evolution occurred in jerks contrary to phyletic gradualism proposed in modern theory. The modern synthetic theory of evolution was developed in 1930 and 1940 and brought out importance of natural selection based on the contributions of genetics, systematics and palaeontology. The geneticists believe that acquired characters are not inherited and genes regulate the phenotypic effects in organisms. The evidences provided by the systematists are that variations within and among the geographic races had a genetic basis and palaeontologists provided evidence that fossil data were consistent with Darwinian theory though he spoke little about human evolution and used to say often ' light will be thrown on the origin of man and his history'.

Q5. What is neo-Darwinism?

Ans. Neo-Darwinism, also called the **modern evolutionary synthesis,** generally denotes the integration of Charles Darwin's theory of evolution by natural selection, Gregor Mendel's theory of genetics as the basis for biological inheritance, and mathematical population genetics. Although this was not the historical meaning of the term neo-Darwinism, it has been the popular and scientific use of the expression since the synthesis of the 1930s. Neo-Darwinism also known as modern synthesis, evolutionary synthesis, and neo-Darwinian synthesis.

Neo-Darwinism has been one of the most significant, overall developments in evolutionary biology since the time of Darwin. Bowler (1988) stated that there is "a sense in which the emergence of the modern synthetic theory can be seen as the first real triumph of Darwinism." Essentially, neo-Darwinism introduced the connection between two important discoveries: the units of evolution (genes) with the mechanism of evolution (natural selection). By melding classical Darwinism with the rediscovered Mendelian genetics, Darwin's ideas were recast in terms of changes in allele frequencies. Neo-Darwinism thus fused two very different and formerly divided research traditions, the Darwinian naturalists and the experimental geneticists.

While the modern synthesis remains the prevailing paradigm of evolutionary biology, in recent years it has both been expanded and challenged as a result of new developments in evolutionary theory. In particular, concepts related to gradualism, speciation, **natural** selection, and extrapolating macroevolutionary trends from microevolutionary trends have been challenged.

Q6. Briefly explain the tenets of Darwin's theory. Why has Darwin's original theory undergone modifications?

Ans. Darwin based his theory of evolution on five observations and three deductions from them and the tenets are as follows:

Observations

Fact-1: The offspring in early stage are numerous than their parents suggests that all organisms tend to increase their number exponentially.

Fact-2: In spite of progressive increase, the number of individuals in a population of a given species remains more or less constant.

Fact-3: Natural resources are limited and remain constant in stable environment.

Inference-1: As more individuals are born than can be supported by the available resources and the size remains stable, there might be 'struggle for existence'. This competition among the individuals results in survival of less number of progeny in each generation.

Fact-4: No two individuals in a given population are identical and display considerable variability in the characteristics of its individuals.

Inference -2: From the 'struggle for existence', some of the variations are advantageous and others unfavourable. Consequently, a higher proportion of individuals with favourable variation on an average will survive whereas a higher proportion of those with unfavourable variations will die or leave the progeny. This unequal survival is the process of natural selection.

Fact-5: Most of the variations are heritable.

Inference-5: Thus, natural selection, in the short run, will act constantly to improve, the adjustments of animals and plants to their surroundings and their ways of life. Over several generations, given the heritable nature of most variations, the process of differential i.e. Unequal survival through natural selection will result in a continuous and gradual change in the characteristics- morphological, physiological- resulting in the population i.e. In the evolution of new species. This observation proves that "Evolution is descent with modification through variation and natural selection".

❏❏❏

CHAPTER-10

THE EVIDENCE FOR EVOLUTION

INTRODUCTION

The evolutionary theory is the basic idea that life has existed for billions of years and has changed over time. Overwhelming evidence supports this fact. Scientists continue to argue about details of evolution, but the question of whether life has a long history or not was answered in the affirmative at least two centuries ago.

The history of living things is documented through multiple lines of evidence that converge to tell the story of life through time. In this unit, we will explore the concept of organic evolution and evidence that are used to reconstruct this story.

Q1. How geological records help in determining the age of rocks? What is radioactive dating?

Or

What is 'radioactive dating'? How does it help in the study of evolution. **[Dec-2019, Q.No.-4 (b)]**

Ans. The geological records are significant to find out the preservations in the earth's crust of living organism in the form of fossil and to establish the great age of the earth. The rock formation has been going on since the birth of the planet and fossilization since the advent of life. The rocks are formed as a result of various geological processes such as erosion, wind action, submergence, elevation, volcanic activity, transportation, physical weathering and climatic changes. With the result of these processes mud, sand or stones are transported to the floor of depressions, lakes or oceans and accumulate there. Materials so deposited later becomes compressed and solidified, forming layers or strata of the rocks entrap the remains of life in the form of fossils.

To determine the age of rocks, two methods were used by the geologists namely: Relative dating and Absolute dating.

- **Relative dating:** the sediments carry remains of plants and animals with them and slowly settle at the bottom of ocean and gradually compacted into layer upon layer of rock. Sedimentary rocks remain undisturbed, the deepest strata is the oldest and recent one is superficial. All strata are deposited sequentially in horizontal layers, deformation may take place at later stage and may tilt or overturn the strata. The thick or fine- grained strata are formed as long and continued deposits and thin or coerce-grained strata are formed due to short period of depositions.

    William Smith noticed that different strata were characterised by different sets of fossils. Older strata lying below and younger strata lying above a given horizon had different fossil. With this discovery it became possible to know the age of the rocks which were miles away from familiar locality and rock type was changed as fossils were same. Fossils are never repeated in the earth's history once the organism is extinct and hence fossils play important role in the estimation of age of rocks.

- **Absolute dating**: The absolute age of rocks and fossil deposits can be estimated by radioactive dating. The radioactive isotopes present in earth's crust decay into stable, nonradioactive elements at well defined constant rate and they form the radioactive clock.

  Radioactive dating is also called as radiometric dating, based on this fact, radioactive isotopes has a characteristic 'half-life' the time taken for one half of a given quantity of radioactive isotope to decay. The half-life of uranium 238 is about 4.5 billion years, the half the molecules of a given amount of uranium will break down forming lead and helium. The final decay product of uranium 238 is lead having 206 atomic weight. Thus, by measuring proportion of parent radioactive material to decay product in a rock sample, the absolute age of the specimen can be calculated.

  Dating with radioactive carbon can be used for any carbon containing material. Living organism utilise a small constant proportion of their organic carbon in the radioactive form. The half-life of radioactive carbon is 5,700 ± 30 years. Hence, the remnants of bone, wood or other carbon-containing remains of dead organisms can be assayed for their radiocarbon content.

  Various techniques are available for dating rocks and hence it is possible to determine the age and fossil contained therein in the range of hundred thousand to a few million years.

Q2. What is fossil? Do you think that fossil record is incomplete? Justify your answer with example.

Ans. Fossil Record are convincing and direct evidence for evolution and are carefully chosen for study as it conveys multiple concepts. Fossils are records of entire organism or part of it. The organism itself may be dissolved, leaving a impression or mould of it which may be filled with deposited material, forming a natural cast or just a footprint or imprint of a leaf on the rock. Paleontologists, geologists, biologists, and others use the fossil record to learn about the past history of the Earth. Using this knowledge, we have gained an understanding of geologic processes that continue today, biodiversity past and present, species origination and extinction, past and present climates, oceans, and atmospheres among others. We have in fact been able to piece together the fascinating story of our dynamic earth for the past 3.5 billion years.

To study any fossil, hard parts are necessary for example, teeth, bones in vertebrates, shells and spicules of invertebrates and woody parts of plants. It is rare to find soft parts preserved in sediments for example in Archeopteryx, only feather impressions have survived.

Fossil records are not complete records as a small fraction of millions of organisms survived as fossil and remaining parts are destroyed. The organisms which were not living in area sedimentations are unlikely to be preserved. The rocks with their fossils may be disturbed and altered in many ways by geological processes.

Fossilization is an infrequent occurrence that is highly dependent on chance. In the past, like today, the remains of most organisms were eaten by animals, consumed by microorganisms, or weathered away. Only dead organisms that are buried in sediment quickly can escape these destructive natural processes and become fossils. After remains have been buried and preserved, they may still be destroyed by geological processes, or exposed and weathered away before people can find them.

Organisms that were very rare in their environment might never have been fossilized simply because the odds of preservation favor more numerous organisms. Animals with small and delicate bones, such as small birds and amphibians, would be less likely to be preserved - and discovered - than larger organisms with tougher bones. Soft-bodied organisms like worms are even more poorly represented in the fossil record because they had no hard parts that could resist decay. We usually learn of their existence only if we find fossilized burrows, or track ways or impressions left by their bodies in soft sediments.

Scientists studying ancient ecosystems such as this one try to collect fossils from as many types of organisms as possible, but they never expect to find fossil evidence of everything that lived there.

Q3. Explain with the help of an example, why there is a marked discontinuity in the geographic distribution of some species.

Ans. It has been observed that closely related organisms may be found in widely separated areas for example Nyssa, the black gum tree naturally occur in South East Asia and eastern North America. These areas have similar physical and biotic environment. Nyssa is not found naturally occurring in the vast area that separate these two regions. Fossil evidence shows that during warmer age this plant and its associated species were distributed over a continuous range that comprised much of the northern hemisphere. During glacial age the climate become severe for plants in most of the area in this range. This is the reason that Nyssa plant is extinct in most parts and survives in milder climate.

We can expect the plant to be present in similar conditions. Such a distribution where pop[ulation of same species are widely separated is called **vicariant.**

Q4. Explain briefly how the presence of vestigial vermiform appendix in humans provides evidence for evolution.

Ans. The presence of **vestigial** or **rudimentary organs** is a proof of our notion of speciation through evolution which shows that vestiges represent structures that were once useful to the ancestors and when evolution got modified afterwards which resulted in adaptations to changed environmental conditions. In many cases the reduced organ has assumed a new function, completely unlike that for which it was originally adapted. In other cases it is apparently useless. The widely known vestigial organs is a human vermiform appendix, a small worm like structure which is a constricted terminal portion of caecum of large intestine. In some mammals it lives on course fibrous diet, made up of a considerable amount of cellulose, the calcium and the appendix are considerably larger. This enables the bacteria present therein to digest cellulose enzymatically.

In humans dietary habits have changed and cellulose intake has been reduced, the appendix has become superfluous and remains rudimentary. Sometimes it creates problem when get enlarge and causes appendicitis, the organ has to be removed by surgery without dire consequences.

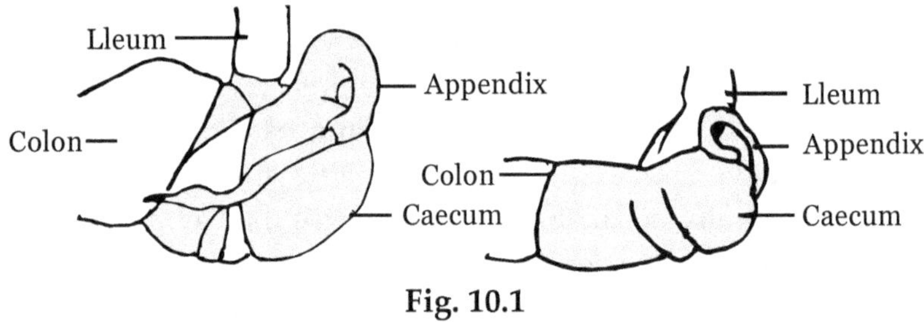

Fig. 10.1

There are many other vestigial organs found in animals and plants for example nictating membrane of the eye, external ear muscles, wisdom tooth in humans, the vestigial caudal vertebrae called embryonic tail in higher primates, the pelvic girdle in whales, boas and pythons, degenerated eyes in cave dwelling vertebrates and invertebrates.

In plants covered stomata on the stem of cactus, vestigial leaf in prickly pears, abortive stamens of Labiates and abortive pistil lodes of male flowers of Cucerbitaceae. In some species of Composite, the ray florets have abortive pistil devoid of any stigma and hence fail in fertilization results into abortive ovules. It is a great example of comparative anatomy which support the organic evolution.

Q5. What is the major criticism of Haeckel's law?

Ans. One of the central, unresolved controversies in biology concerns the distribution of primitive versus advanced characters at different stages of vertebrate development. This controversy has major implications for evolutionary developmental biology and phylogenetics. Ernst Haeckel addressed the issue with his Biogenetic

Law, and his embryo drawings functioned as supporting data. The embryological evidence for organic evolution become prominence with the recapitulation theory or Biogenetic Law of Haeckel's where comparative embryology was evolutionary but non-quantitative. It was based on developmental sequences, and treated heterochrony as a sequence change. It is not always clear whether he believed in recapitulation of single characters or entire stages. The **Biogenetic Law** is supported by several recent studies -- if applied to single characters only. Haeckel's important but overlooked alphabetical analogy of evolution and development is an advance on von Baer. Haeckel recognized the evolutionary diversity in early embryonic stages, in line with modern thinking. He did not necessarily advocate the strict form of recapitulation and terminal addition commonly attributed to him. Haeckel's much-criticized embryo drawings are important as phylogenetic hypotheses, teaching aids, and evidence for evolution. While some criticisms of the drawings are legitimate, others are more tendentious. In opposition to Haeckel and his embryo drawings, Wilhelm has made major advances towards developing a quantitative comparative embryology based on morphometrics. Unfortunately his work in this area is largely forgotten. Despite his obvious flaws, Haeckel can be seen as the father of a sequence-based phylogenetic embryology.

As shown in the figure below an example of Crustaceans, the larvae pass through six distinct stages in successive moults, each larval stage resembles the adult from primitive to advanced form. The larvae of primitive crustaceans stop growth and differentiation at an early stage whereas the advanced crustaceans show all or most of the stages as shown in the figure below:

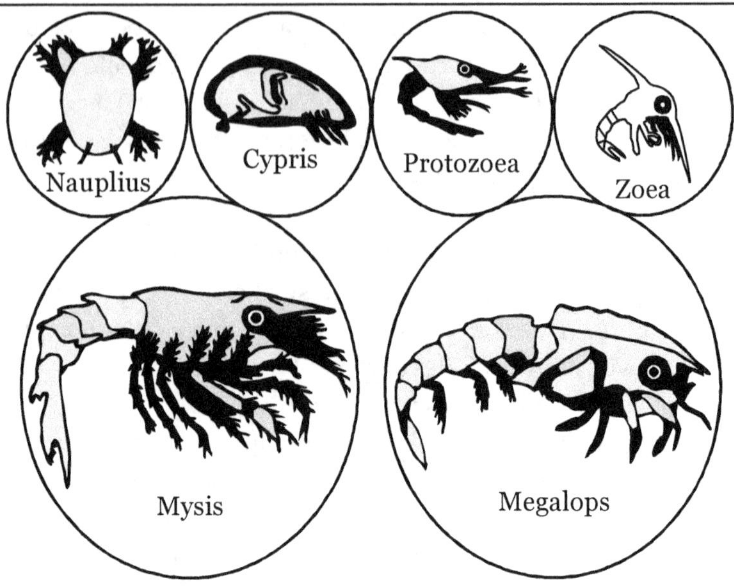

Fig. 10.2

Q6.   Discuss the development of embryos of different vertebrates as evidence of recapitulation.

Ans. The embryos of different vertebrates show a high degree of similarities at various stages of development and become different morphologically during the later stages of growth. Haeckel's biogenetic law was criticised as there is no true phylogenetic recapitulation during ontogeny and this is because the resemblances seen in ontogeny are primarily between embryos or related animals and not among embryos and adult ancestors. The ontogeny recapitulates phylogeny only in the sense that ancestral embryonic stages are repeated and may be drastically modified by adaptations that are favoured by natural selection.

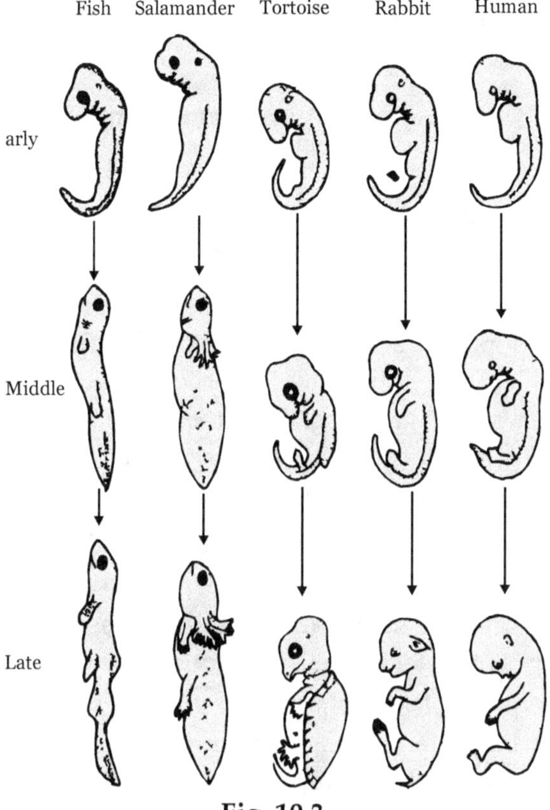

Fig. 10.3

The recapitulation theory assumes that embryos need only repeat the past, condensing some stages and eleminating others without adapting to the embryonic mode of life and adapt themselves to cope up with a hostile environment like adults. The differences in cleavage pattern in various embryos are correlated with the amount of yolk in the eggs. This is an adaptive trait of fundamental biological importance. Several studies have done to consider the adaptations of eggs in order to develop in fresh water, salt water or terrestrial habitats. There are significant differences among various groups of echinoderms which are referable to embryonic adaptations. Many biologists feel that these differences are result of extensive modifications of larvae through natural selection, since separation from their ancestors.

Q7. What is von Baer's Principle?

Or

List Von Baer's four principles of embryonic differentiation.

[Dec-2019, Q.No.-2 (a)]

Ans. The observation of Haeckel on von Baer's Principles of embryonic differentiation is based on:

- The characters that are observed during embryological development are typical of the particular phylogenetic line i.e. 'general' characters precedes those characteristics of species itself i.e. 'special' characters.
- The progression from the more general to less general and finally to the special characters during development.
- An animal during its development departs progressively from the forms of other related species.
- The juvenile stages of an animal resemble the embryonic stages of lower animals but not those of adults.
- The principles of embryonic differentiation put forward by von Baer are better guide to the interpretation of evidence from embryology supportive of organic evolution.

Q8. What is comparative serology? Outline the major steps involved in a precipitin test.

Ans. The comparative biochemistry gives the insight of many synthetic and degradative pathways to most organism whether closely or distantly related. All organisms depend on carbohydrates and fats and to some extent protein for energy and the common pathway is glycolytic cycle, TCA cycle and the electron transport chain in most of the organisms.

Comparative serology provides evidence for evolution based on the fact that animal will form antibodies against complex compounds like protein which is foreign to that animal's body. The substance which induce the formation of antibodies is called an antigen. If a small amount of serum of any animal is injected into another test animal, the foreign serum acts as an antigen and causes the production of circulating antibodies in test animal.

Suppose an antiserum is prepared and we add few drops of original antigenic serum, precipitate is formed. This type of antibody forming mechanism is called immune mechanism. With this process, we immunised the test animal against the kind of serum that was injected. The antibodies that react with the antigen to form a precipitate called precipitating antibodies and the test is called **precipitin test**.

For example a rabbit is injected with human serum to immunised it against human serum and form antibodies against it. The antiserum obtained from the rabbit's blood containing antibodies against human serum now serves as test fluid and is divided into four test tubes as shown in figure below:

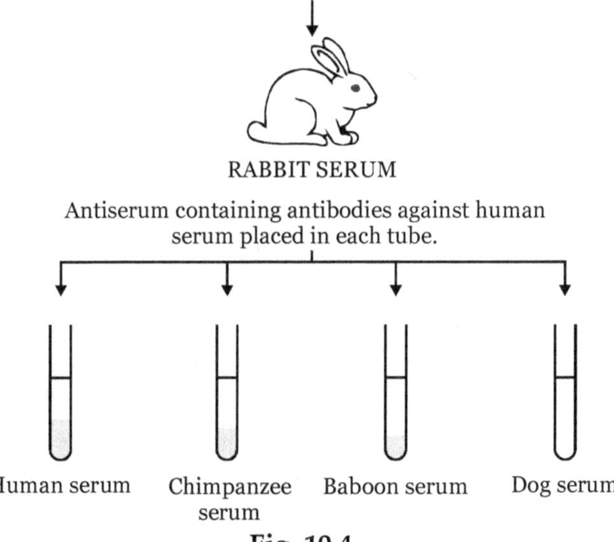

Fig. 10.4

As shown in the figure test tube-1 antiserum is mixed with human serum. Antigen-antibody reaction will occur and a soft white precipitate will be formed and settle down at the bottom of the tube. In test tube-2 antiserum is mixed with chimpanzee serum. The antigen-antibody reaction depend upon whether or not protein of chimpanzee serum are similar in chemical structure of human serum. If similar than antibodies formed against one will also react with other. The results of test tube 1 and 2 shows that chimpanzee serum is homologous to human serum.

If we mix antiserum with baboon serum, a small amount of precipitate will be formed as shown in test tube-3. This is because the representative proteins in baboon serum is not similar to human serum proteins and we do not get the precipitin reaction.

If we mix antiserum with dog serum as shown in test tube-4, no precipitate is formed, which indicates that dog serum is different from human serum protein and do not react with antihuman serum antibodies. The experiment show the degree of relationship amongst the various organisms and results so obtained based on comparative morphology.

Q9. What do you mean by amino acid sequences and nucleic acid hybridisation?

Ans. Proteins are determined to relate the various species. To understand this cytochrome C is an example of respiratory pigment, an essential component of mitochondrial electron transport system has been used.

The cytoghrome C is a single polypeptide-chain composed of 104 amino acids in mammals. Amino acid sequence of cytochrome C has been detetrmined on 67 plants and animal species i.e. from yeast and fungi to humans. Certain amino acids occupy specific position in polypeptide chain are invarient which shows amino acids are essential for the function of proteins at its specific position. At many positions on polypeptide chain where amino acid can be replaced by another without affecting the biological activity of protein.

If we study phylogeny of cytochrome C, we find different species have different cytochrome C sequences occur only in amino acids whose replacement does nogt affect its activity. Closely related species differ from one another by fewer amino acid residues than distantly related species though cytochrome C in all these forms indicates common ancestry as shown in the evolutionary tree below which shows that phylogenetic classification is based on morphological structure.

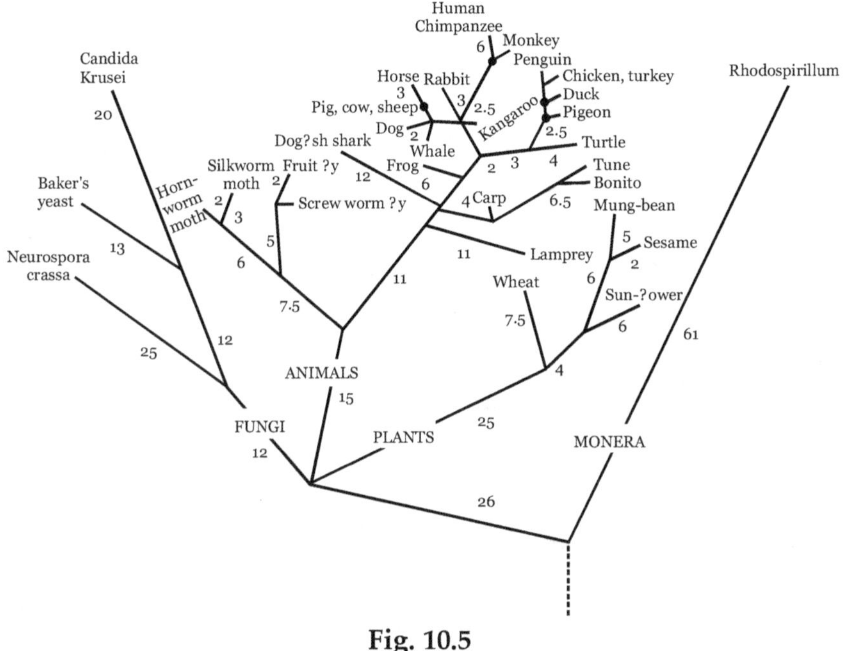

Fig. 10.5

Nucleic acid hybridisation is biochemical study to trace molecular phylogeny. In this method DNA is extracted from a test species-A for example human volunteer. The double stranded molecule is separated by heating into single strand, which are then trapped into blocks of gel so that on cooling complementary chains do not join. The DNA from species-B labelled with radioactive phosphorus are also separated in to single strand and passed throgh gel blocks containing strands of species-A. Now the portions of strands of species A and B which are complementary to each other will unite to form double strands. Now it is possible to separately recover the uncombined fraction as well as double stranded DNA which can be estimated quantitatively. It can be observed that the closer the relationship between the organism, the greater the proportion of double stranded DNA samples obtained from the gel. This enable us to form a phylogenetic tree and support the theory of evolution.

Q10. Distinguish between homologous and analogous organs.

Or

Write a short note on Honologous organs. [Dec-2019, Q.No.-6 (c)]

Ans. Homologous organs have similar embryonic origin and basic structure whereas Analogous organs have different embryonic origin and basic structure. Homologous organs may look different and may perform different function; e.g., forelimb of a man and flipper of a whale. Whereas Analogous organs look alike and perform same functions; e.g., Wings of birds and insects.

Table 10.1

Homologous Organs	Analogous Organs
Adapted for different functions	Adapted for similar functions
Similar basic plan and origin	Different body plan and origin
It is due to divergent evolution	It is due to convergent evolution
It indicates evolutionary relationship	It does not indicate evolutionary relationship
Example: Forelimbs of vertebrates	Example: Wings of insect and birds

Q11. Write short note on Geological Time Scale.

Ans. Palaeontologists have established a geological chronology on the basis of stratigraphical data and divided the age of the earth into different eras, period and epochs. They have been able to estimate the relative lengths of various geological periods in terms of million of years. The fossil record from different strata reveals the time when the major groups of organisms appeared and the idea of possible ancestors and close relatives of some modern species.

The eras, periods and epochs are arranged on time scale and the arrangement is called **Geological time scale** as shown in the table below which reveals many facts of evolution like inhabitants of a given period are descended from a part and not all inhabitants of earlier period. It also reveals that many species and genera disappeared from the scene without leaving the descendents and become extinct.

Table 10.2

Era	Period	Epoch	Time from beginning 10 present (Millions of years)	Geological Condilions	Biological Features
Cenozoic (Era of Modern Life) (Age of Mammals)	Quarter-nary	Recent	0.025	End of 4th ice age, climate warmer	Modem man, mammals, birds, fishes, insects.
		Pleistocene	1	Four ice ages, climate cold and mild	Extinction of great mammals: Primitive man common.
	Tertiary	Pliocene	10	Volcanic activity, climate dry and cool	Emergence of man from man-like apes; Formation of modem mammals.
		Miocene	25	Development of plains and grasslands,	Mammals at peak, First man-like apes

				climate moderate	formed.
		Oligoce ne	40	Mountain building, climate mild	Extinction of archaic, mammals. Rise of first monkeys and apes, and ancestors of modern mammals.
		Eocene	60	Mountain erosion, heavy rainfall, climate warmer.	Diversifica tion of placental mammals.
		Palaeoce ne	70	Mountain building, climate cool to moderate	Dominanc e of archaic mammals; rise of first primates, placental mammals and modern birds.
Mesozoic (Era of Medieval Life)	Cretaceou s		135	Spread of inland seas and swamps, Mountains (Andes,	Extinction of giant reptiles and toothed birds; Rise

				Himalayas, Alps, Rocky, etc.) formed.	of first modern birds; Archaic mammals common.
	Jurassic		180	Continents fairly high, shallow seas over part of Europe and USA	Rise of first toothed birds; Reptiles dominant; Dinosaurs became large.
(Age of reptiles)	Triassic		230	Continents elevated, widespread deserts	Rise of first dinosaurs and egg laying mammals; Extinction of primitive amphibians.
Palaeozoic (Era of Ancient life) (Age of	Permian		270	Rise of continents, increasing glaciation, cool dry climate	Extinction of many marine invertebrates; Rise of modern insects, spread of reptilies.

Amphi-bians)	Carbonife rous		350	Increase in inland seas and mountains, climate first warm later cool.	Origin of reptiles and winged insects; spread of sharks and amphibian s; crinoids at peak.
(Age of Fishes)	Devonian		400	Formation of inland seas and mountains, lands higher	Origin of amphibian sand forests; fishesabun dant
	Silurian		40	Rise of lands, relatively flat continents, climate mild	Origin of jawed fishes and wingless insects; invasion of land by arthropods and plants.
(Age of invertebr ates)	Ordovicia n		500	Submergen ce of lands, expansion of oceans, climate warm even in arctic	Origin of vertebrates (jawless armoured fishes); invertebrat es abundant.
	Cambrian		600	Lands low, climate mild	All invertebrat e phyla

					established ; trilobitesa nd brachiopo ds dominant.
Proterozo ic (Era of Early Life)			2,000	Great sedimentat ion, volcanic activity, extensive erosion, repeated glaciation, climate warm-most to cool-dry	Origin of simple marine invertebrat es without shell; scanty fossils.
Areheozo ic (Era of Primitive life).	Precambri an		3,600	Great volcanicact ivity, some sedimentat ion, extensive erosion	Origin of life; no recognizab le fossils.

Q12. Describe evolutionary trends in horse. Enumerate the two major changes that took place in the history of evolution of modern horse.

Or

Give a brief account of evolution of horse.

[June-2019, Q.No.-6 (b)]

Ans. The phylogeny of the horse was deduced from the fossil record which shows that during the evolution every part of the horse skeleton was affected. The major changes during long evolutionary history was seen as enumerated below:

- General increase in size.
- Enlargement of cerebral hemisphere of brain and increase in the head size.
- Increased length and mobility of the neck.
- Increase in height and complexity of molar teeth.
- Enlargement of last two and finally the last three premolars untill they are comparable to the molars.
- Elongation of limbs for speedy running but with a loss of rotational movement.
- Fusion of bones in the limbs to provide better hinge joints for more efficient support of body weight.
- Reduction of toes from five to one long toe (third) on each foot covered by a hoof or claw. The lateral toes are gradually reduced and finally only small bones of the second and fourth toe persist as splints.

With these evolutionary changes the horse became long-legged, swift-running mammal adapted to live and feed on open grasslands. The prominent teeth having many enamel ridges help in grinding tough grassy vegetation.

Q13. "Most of the species on oceanic islands are endemic" Explain.

Ans. Darwin observed during one of his voyage in Beagle island that oceanic islands lying beyond continents having much less number of naturally occurring species of organisms. He found that many of the species are endemic on this island and are not found anywhere else.

Darwin found 26 species of land birds in the Galapagos archipelago island. Of these 21 to 23 species were found to be endemic but out of 11 species of marine birds, 2 were endemic. The head and beak of the birds have different structure and also have different feeding habits which enable them to occupy different ecological niches within restricted area. The Galapagos island include 436 species, of which 223 are endemic and are restricted to few islands in archipelago. As the island struck by the endemic nature of flora and fauna, Darwin proposed that islands were colonised by occasional migrants from the mainland. He proposed to isolate population and modify them by forming groups of closely related endemic species. The wide water barrier would greatly reduce the spreading to other localities. For marine birds, such a barrier is less formidable and we find smaller proportion of endemics amongst the marine birds.

Many animals and plants known to humans on these islands survived and multiplied successfully and hence this proves these islands are well suited to support greater variety of organisms.

The amphibians and terrestrial mammals not bats are entirely absent from oceanic islands. They multiply rapidly to become nuisance. The toad, *Bufo marinus* was introduced to control insects in Hawaii but now they have become nuisance on the island. All species been created in the places in which they exist now, then amphibians and terrestrial mammals would be as frequent on oceanic islands as on comparatively similar continental areas.

CHAPTER 11

THE PROCESS OF EVOLUTIONARY CHANGE

INTRODUCTION

Evolutionary theories are based on the assumption that societies gradually change from simple beginnings into even more complex forms. Early sociologists beginning with Auguste Comte believed that human societies evolve in a unilinear way- that is in one line of development. This evolutionary view of social change was highly influenced by Charles Darwin's theory of Organic Evolution. Theodosius Dobzhansky, a geneticist who was one of the trinity to structure the modern synthetic theory of evolution stated " Nothing in Biology makes sense, except in the light of evolution". This unit will highlight that natural selection promotes structural, functional and ecological adaptations of individuals, populations and species to their existing environment.

Q1. What are different basis of natural selection? Explain.

Ans. Natural selection is the gradual process by which heritable biological traits become either more or less common in a population as a function of the effect of inherited traits on the differential reproductive success of organisms interacting with their environment. It is a key mechanism of evolution. The term "natural selection" was popularised by Charles Darwin, who intended it to be compared with artificial selection, now more commonly referred to as selective breeding.

The different basis of natural selection are:

- **The Prodigality of Nature:** This means that an organism has potential to reproduce. For example a frog can lay as many as 12,000 eggs and if all the eggs survive and reproduce, then entire earth will be strewn with frogs. On other hand an elephant is a slow breeder and during its 100 years of existence gives birth to six calves in 60 years of its reproductive life. There can be 19 million elephants in around 750 years. So these example shows that animals have immence potential for reproduction.

  The number of most of the species are are always maintained at optimal level otherwise lakes would have been choked with fishes and fields would have been strewn with frogs. This is because various limiting factors in the environment both biotic and abiotic keep a check on the increase in numbers.

- **Factors that limit the Reproductive Potential:** The organisms have to compete for their survival in the form of food, territory, adverse climate, escape from predators or to combat infections. This the struggle for existence which manage the population. In some some other population, the number increases dramatically in certain seasons and decrease in other seasons. In laboratory one can grow cell culture in one of the resources such as food, space etc. Under such circumstances the population growth rate of the cells which is exponential to begin with decreases and levels off.

The resulting sigmoid curve is characteristic of biological growth in general as shown in figure.

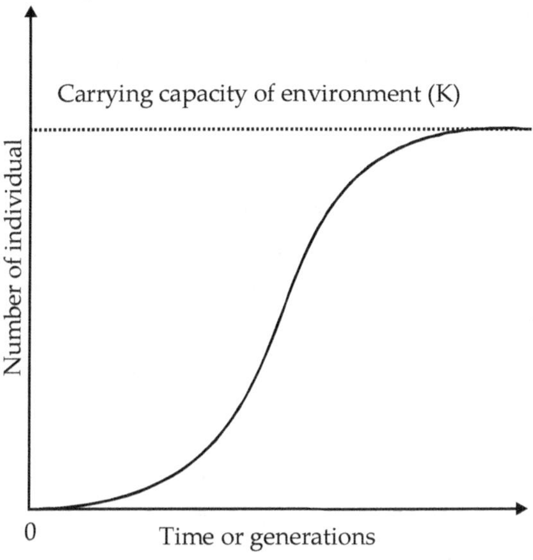

Fig. 11.1

These factors delimit the numbersor size to the carrying capacity of the environment in natural population. The carrying capacity of the environment for plants is controlled by the amount of space required by the individuals of their own and other species. No new seeds or shoots can develop in that particular area until the older plants fall. Population size can be limited by food supply. If certain proportion is able to overcome struggle and survive to produce next offspring, this chance alone determines which individual should survive and which one should die.

- **Variability in population:** "The variation of animals and plants under domestication" is a book written by Darwin where he pointed out that the population of living organism are not composed of identical individuals.

It is true that monozygotic twins may express differences between them which can be identified in different traits in a population.

There are chances that change in environment which is adverse to the organism would wipe out the entire population. So, in the absence of variability, there may not be any evolutionary change. The major source is genetic variability in organisms caused by mutations of all kinds which results in Drosophila may have normal or vestigial wings or red or white eyes. Sweet peas may have red or white flowers and individuals with blood groups A or B or AB or O having black or brown or blue eyes so omn amnd so forth. The subtle effects of environment add another dimension to the variability of traits in natural population.

- **Natural selection:** It is the gradual process by which heritable biological traits become either more or less common in a population as a function of the effect of inherited traits on the differential reproductive success of organisms interacting with their environment. It is a key mechanism of evolution.

- Natural selection is Darwin's most famous theory; it states that evolutionary change comes through the production of variation in each generation and differential survival of individuals with different combinations of these variable characters. Individuals with characteristics which increase their probability of survival will have more opportunities to reproduce and their offspring will also benefit from the heritable, advantageous character. So over time these variants will spread through the population.

Q2. How do you justify the statement that natural selection is synonymous with differential reproduction?

Ans. Darwin proposed the theory of natural selection which states that genetic variations produced as adaptations to changing environment are pre-requisites for the survival of the organisms. If an individual has some trait which gives him better chance of survival in a given environment, it is evident that offspring will inherit that trait and this is known as differential survival referred as survival of individuals in a well adapted environment. The individuals who do not possess such adaptations may not survive to reproduce. The adaptations are genetically controlled and heritable. Differential survival leads to differential reproduction of alleles responsible for the survival of next generation. Hence this justifies the statement that natural selection is synonymous with differential reproduction.

Q3. If the heritable variability does not exist in populations, could there have been an evolutionary process?

Ans. The differences in heritable traits exhibited by an individual species is said to be variability. Darwin in his book 'The variation of animals and plants under domestication' have said that population of living organisms are not composed of identical individuals. If heritable variability does not exist in population, than chance would decide which organism will survive and which would not. In the absence of variability, all organisms in population would be uniform. There are chances that change in environment which is adverse to the organism would wipe out the entire population. So, in the absence of variability, there may not be any evolutionary change. The major source is genetic variability in organisms caused by mutations of all kinds which results in Drosophila may have normal or vestigial wings or red or white eyes. Sweet peas may have red or white flowers and individuals with blood groups A or B or AB or O having black or brown or blue eyes so omn amnd so forth. The subtle effects of environment add another dimension to the variability of traits in natural population.

Q4. What is meant by the term fitness value? Assuming that the selection coefficient of a genotype is 0.35, what is the fitness value of the genotype?

Ans. It can be defined either with respect to a genotype or phenotype. In either case, it describes the ability to both survive and reproduce, and is equal to the average contribution to the gene pool of the next generation that is made by an average individual of the specified genotype or phenotype. The term "Darwinian fitness" is often used to make clear the distinction with physical fitness. If differences between alleles of a given gene affect Darwinian fitness, then the frequencies of the alleles will change across generations; the alleles with higher fitness become more common. This process is called natural selection.

The fitness value quantifies the relative reproductive efficiency of a genotype with reference to another genotype. If s, the selection coefficient of genotype is 0.35, then w, the fitness value of genotype is 1-0.35 = 0.65.

Q5. What is the type of selection operating in African population in maintaining the heterozygous genotypes HbA/HbS at higher frequency? (HbA– allele for normal hemoglobin and HbS– allele for sickle cell haemoglobin).

Ans. In African population the selection maintains the heterozygous genotypes HbA/HbS at high frequency but two homozygotes are not favoured for two reasons: The HbS/HbS genotype causes the sickle cell disease and the patient homozygous for HbS die early because of lysis of erythrocytes.

The HbA/HbA homozygotes are susceptible to falciparum malaria. In heterozygotes where an HbS allele is present, there is sickling of cells to some extent but genotypes rexhibit resistance to malaria. Since both the homozygotes are selected against and only heterozygotes favoured. It is the normalising selection which is operating in African population. Sickle cell anaemia is an example where having a defective allele or part of the genotype proves to be an adaptation.

Q6. What are the sources and expression of variability?

Or

Define Aneuploidy.   **[Dec-2019, Q.No.-1 (b) (ii)]**

Ans. Mutations and genetic recombination in sexually reproducing organisms are major sources of variation in natural population. The different forms of mutations as a source of variability are:

(I) Mutations: This is the process by which change arise in the genetic material and the end product. The mutation form separate category of source of variability distinct from genetic recombination or indepemdent assortment of chromosomes, characteristic of sexually reproducing individuals. There are two forms of mutation:

Chromosomal mutation: Affect the number of chromosomes and number of arrangement of genes in a chromosome. Following are the ways in which chromosomal mutations occur:

(i) **Changes in the arrangement of genes.**

   (a) **Deficiency or deletion:** Refers to the loss of a segment of chromosome containing one or several genes.

   (b) **Duplication**: Refers to occurrence of more than once of one or more genes in a chromosomes. Duplication occur random i.e. Two or more duplicated segments may lie adjacent to each other on the same chromosome.

(ii) **Changes in arrangement of genes in a chromosome**

   (a) **Inversion:** The given sequence within segment of chromosome is reverted

   (b) **Translocation:** The location of block of genes is changed in the chromosome. Tranlocation is reciprocal i.e. An exchange of a block of gnes between two non-homologous chromosomes

(iii) **Changes in chromosome number**

   (a) **Aneuploidy:** One or more chromosomes of a normal set may be lacking or present in excess. The nullisomy refers to absence of both the chromosomes of a pair. Monosomy, trisomy, tetrasomy refer to occurrence of chromosome ones, twice thrice and so on respectively in a diploid organism

   (b) **Polyploidy**: Refer to more than two sets of chromosome in individual. Most organisms are diploid that is they have two sets of chromosomes in somatic cells but one in gametic cell, in polyploid organism is triploid having three sets of chromosome, in tetraploid four sets and so on. Polyploidy occurs in plants and rarely ion animals. Many plants like wheat, oats, tobacco, potato, banana etc. and some flowering plants are polyploid. Polyploidy is sometimes artificialy induced to create new variety. It is one of the means in bisexual organism by which new species could arise

(2) Gene Mutation: Affect only one or a few nucleotides in a gene. This mutation occur when the DNA sequence of gene is altered and new nucleotide sequence is passed to offspring. Nucleotide substitution can be either transitions or transversions. In transition purine replaced by another purine(A by G or vice versa) or pyrimidine by another pyrimidine (C by T or vice versa). Transversions are replacement of purine by pyrimidine or vice versa (G or A by C or T or vice versa)

Different types of gene mutations are:

(i) **Substitutions**: Substitution by one base by another would result in altered amino acid in a polypeptide chain. For instance triplet AAT in DNA (UUA in mRNA) would specify leucine. If the first A is replaced by C, it will code for valine. Some codons degenerate and substitution may not alter the amino acid coded would still be leucine. Gene mutation do not normally affect protein and alter biological function. But nucleotide affect adversely when substitution that change triplet coding for amino acid into a termination codon. In AAT, if second A is replaced by T (ATT), the resulting mRNA codon UAA is a termination codon which if present in the middle of mRNA molecule, the subsequent codons are not translated and incomplete polypeptide will be released from ribosomes.

(ii) **Additions and Deletions:** In the coded polypeptide, the addition and deletion of nucleotide pair in DNA sequence of structural gene often result in altered sequence of amino acid.

DNA sequence look like-CAT-CAT-CAT-CAT-CAT

If nucletide T to be inserted immediately after the first C, the sequence will look like--CTA-TCA-TCA-TCA-TCA-T

The original DNA sequence when transcribed and translated would yield five successive valine residues and altered sequence would read one aspartate and four serine residues. This mutation is called frame shift mutation.

(iii) Mutation rate: every gene has a characteristic mutation rate described on average per gene basis. Drosophila has one detectable mutation per 10,000 loci i.e. 0.01% per locus. In humans some dominant lethal genes like retinoblastoma, chondrodystrophy and Huntington, s chorea have rates varying g from 0.01 to 0.001% per locus that means 10,000 or 100,000 loci mutations. In eukaryotic, mutation rate is 10-4 ton 10-6/loci and in prokaryotic the rate is much lower 10-7 to 10-10/loci. Mutation can occur in reverse direction i.e. Mutant gene can mutate back to its wild form but rate of this mutation is much lower than forward mutation.

(iv) Genetic recombination: Variability generating mechanism is caused by mutation in prokaryotes and asexually reproducing organisms but in eukaryotes, sexual recombination occurs, even in one generation there is marked reshuffling of genes in chromosomes, which amplifies genetic variability in population. Thus, greatest and fundamental advantage of sexual reproduction in the generation of variability, provided population is large even if mutations do not exist, the mechanism of sexual recombination alone would be generating new genotypes for very long time.

Q7. Discuss the action of natural selection in uniform and changing environments.

Or

With the help of an example, discuss how action of natural selection is influenced by the changing environment.

[Dec-2019, Q.No.-2 (b)]

Ans. Action of natural selection in uniform environment: The action of natural selection is seen when there is absence of large scale environmental change and population maintains a uniform environment and genetic constitution or genetic homeostasis. The phenomenon is known as normalising selection.

The phenotypic traits of individuals can be arranged on a linear scale and can be seen in figure a, the distribution curve of the traits usually takes a bell shape, where number of individuals is greater at intermediate values and gradually decrease towards the extreme as shown in figure A. The normalising selection occurs when individuals with intermediate phenotypes are favoured and those with extremes are under selection pressure as shown in figure B. This tendency is seen generation after generation. If there is strong selection pressure against the phenotypes occupying the extremes of normal curve, then the population may show less variability though mean remains the same as shown in figure C. Natural selection has normalising or stabilising effect on populations with mid-values for the traits and individuals with intermediate values for their traits have better chances of survival. For example, new born infants with very less or more than average weight have high rate of mortality than of intermediate weight have less problem of survival.

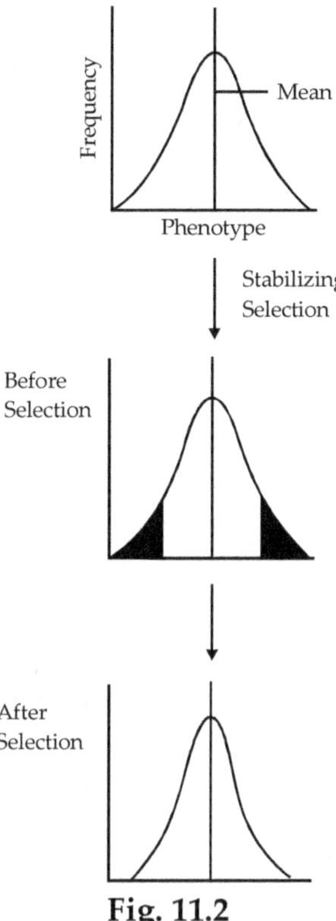

Fig. 11.2

The experiments from nature and Dobzhansky and Spassky explain the concept of normalising selection:

- **Observation of Bumpus:** He collected 136 injured house sparrow after a severe snow and sleet storm with high winds at woods hole. Of these 64 birds died and those survived the storm. Bumpus randomly chose traits like wing length, wing span and tarsus length etc. and found that those killed had measurements which fell at the ends of bell shaped curve and he found that birds with mean or close to mean survive. The normalising selection generally eliminates during a catastrophe or a stressful situation individuals whose traits vary markedly from the mean values. Bumpus also observed that birds which were blown down easily by the winds had either their wings too long for their body weight and therefore presented a larger surface area or they had too short wings for their body size and therefore could not fly against strong winds. Prior to the catastrophe the range of individual measurements was larger as compared to the range of measurements that survived the catastrophe.

- **Experiments of Dobzhansky and Spassky:** They demonstrated the working of normalising selection on the behavioural trait in two population of *Drosophila pseudobsura* which were subject to artificial selection. One population was selected as positive phototactic and other negative phototactic behaviour. Flies were placed in a container from where they could go towards light or darkness. The flies which moved towards light were collected and bred as also the ones which exhibited photonegative which move away from light. The experiment was repeated generation after generation, the artificial selection which is once terminated natural selection favoured individuals with neutral behaviour towards light, the both populations reverted back to an intermediate photo-tactic score as shown in figure below:

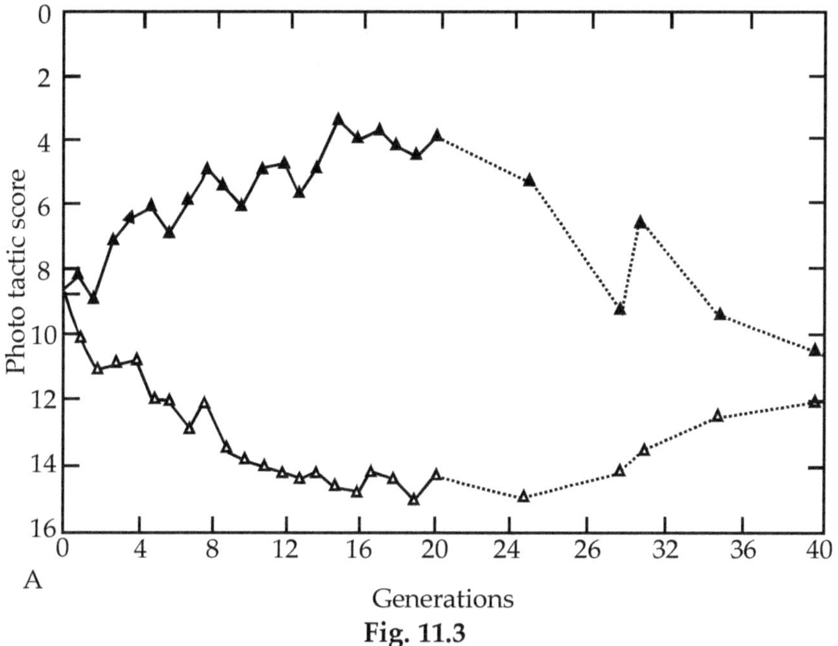

Fig. 11.3

Action of natural selection in changing environments

Directional or progressive selection: This is the mode of selection associated with environmental change where in these circumstances the selection would weed out the individuals from the two ends of normal curve unequally as shown in the figure B. This in turn shifts the mean of trait to new favoured extreme as shown in figure C. With this we observe that directional selection is a modified form of stabilising selection in that it does not work evenly at both ends of the distribution curve.

The example reveals that the directional selection in operation is the ability of pest populations to develop resistance to pesticides. Man is responsible for change in environment and to adapt the changes organisms respond rapidly through directional selection. The first report on resistance to DDT was observed in houseflies in 1947. Finally pesticides become ineffective despite increasing of its concentration.

In every generation more and more insects that exhibit a higher resistance to the pesticide are selected. Pesticides resistance by insects reflects the efficacy of directional selection since these are normally synthetic substances and insects are never exposed to it in natural environment.

Industrial melanism is example of directional selection in changing environment where a species of melanic moths escaping predation because of altered environment.

CHAPTER-12

NATURAL SELECTION IN ACTION

INTRODUCTION

Natural selection is the process by which species adapt to their environment. Natural selection leads to evolutionary change when individuals with certain characteristics have a greater survival or reproductive rate than other individuals in a population and pass on these inheritable genetic characteristics to their offspring. Simply put, natural selection is a consistent difference in survival and reproduction between different genotypes, or even different genes, in what we could call reproductive success.

The role of natural selection in evolving adaptations in individuals belonging to related as well as entirely unrelated species. This unit will illustrate examples of the positive role played by natural selection in perfecting adaptations of competing species occupying a similar environment and in evolving various types of relationship between species having different levels in a food chain. Besides this discuss the concept of sexual selection, kin selection and group selection and their evolutionary implications.

Q1. Distinguish the terms intra- and interspecific competition. Briefly explain that interspecific competition results in the evolution of coadapted communities.

Ans. The resources such as space, nutrients, and water are limited and this will automatically result in the process called **competition**. Competition occurs when organisms have an adverse effect on each other as a result of requiring the same resource.

Competition occurs between two or more organisms. When these organisms belong to the same species it is referred to as **intraspecific** competition. When it occurs between individuals of different species it is **interspecific** competition.

In intraspecific competition, the individuals belonging to same species compete among themselves for the same requisites from the environment which results in physical competition including competition for mates and another component is the individual belonging to species may compete as to which of them leaves behind a major share of descendents in the future population. The second type is more subtle which means that individuals do not compete directly or in physical way and its success is measured in terms of the survival of offspring and alleles in the next generation. Two types of competitions are interrelated, the first type of competition is known as ecological intraspecific competition is a prerequisite for success in the second type of competition namely reproductive intraspecific competition which results in adaptations to a given environment and this helps to perpetuate the genotypes of successful individuals generation after generation.

Interspecific competition is between individuals belonging to different species which do not interbreed. Closely related species do compete for similar requirements from the environment, especially when the niches they occupy tend to overlap and at this time the competition takes place at ecological level.there is no competition for mates but each species would independently try to leave behind a major share of descendents in the population.

Q2. What do you understand by the term character displacement? Describe with a suitable example that character displacement is the outcome of interspecific competition.

Ans. The divergence of two species living in a niche with respect to a character owing to competition between them is referred as character displacement.

To understand this let us consider two species of organisms, species A and B where A species has a population in a community and species B arrives into same community suddenly or brought by man and food organism of both species are same may be any insect or seed. The range of food particle size fed upon by each species falls into a normal curve i.e. There is variation in the given trait for example size of seeds or insects or beak sizes which are all distributed in such a way that the largest number of individuals have extreme sizes or measurement as shown in figure below:

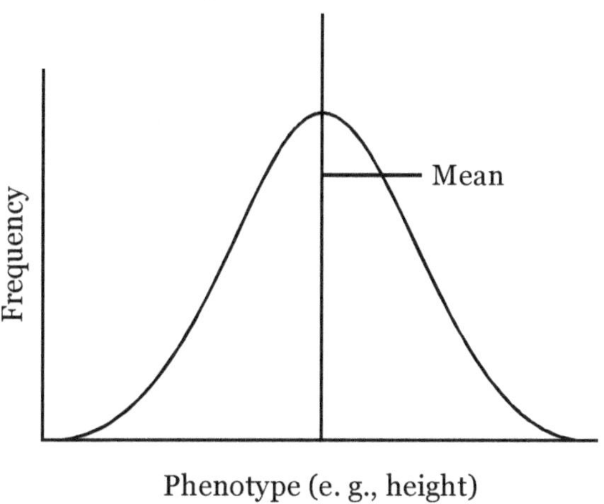

Fig. 12.1

There is a significant overlap in the normal curves of food capturing devices like mouth, beak or tooth sizes of species A and B. There is a ecological interspecific competition for food. Assuming that numbers of food particles are of same size, then the individuals outside the region of overlap have more energy for reproduction and will tend to leave more offsprings to next generation. The offspring will carry alleles of their parents including those involved in the determination of food particle size. The effect of natural selection process over the number generations will be to move the normal curves of foog particle size of two species as shown in the figure below. The two species become adapted to each other's presence in the community or in other words coadapted. The phenomenon of divergence in a character is known character displacement. The phenomenon of separation of niche is referred as ecological exclusion and they are the basis of evolution of coadapted communities.

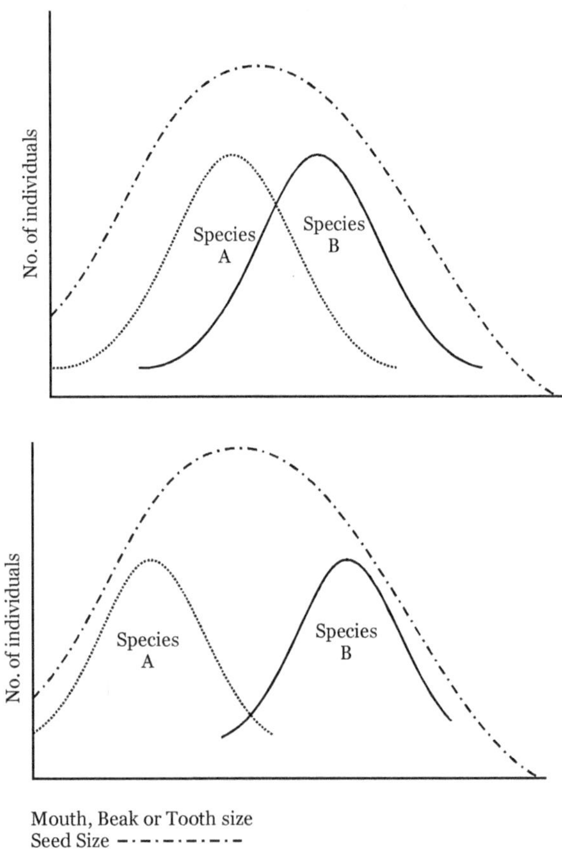

Fig. 12.2

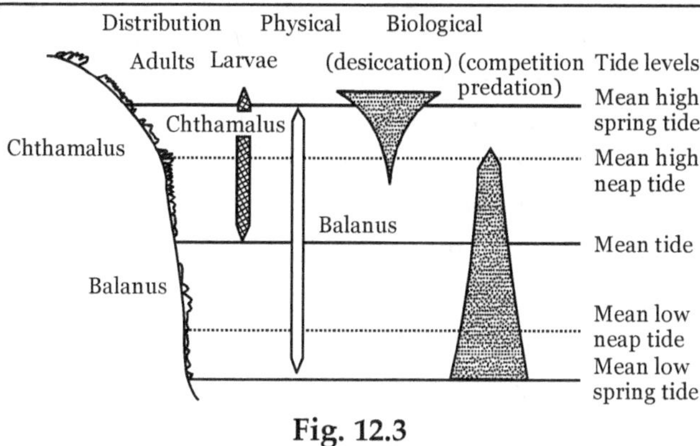

Fig. 12.3

Q3. Briefly explain the concept of coevolution and elaborate the concept with a suitable host parasite relationship example.

Or

What is coevolution? Explain with the example of coevolution of prey and predators or of plants and herbivores.

[June-2019, Q.No.-4(a)]

Ans. The phenomenon which results from a biological interaction between two species which occupy two different levels in a food chain is referred as coevolution which signifies coordinated evolution of two or more species. The coevolutionary relationship between parasites and host can be complicated between predators and their pray as it is expected from host to evolve effective defense mechanism against parasite which in turn should be more virulent. A balance has to be done as parasite cannot afford to increase its own reproductive efficiency at the expense of host. The death of the host is death of the parasite if it is not transmitted to another living host. If the parasite has to be transferred to another host, a parasite must evolve a lower degree of virulence so not to kill the host. A successful host-parasite relationship is evolved on the dictum of " live and let live".

To understand the concept, the coevolution between rabbit as host and myxoma as parasite is considered and found that in ten years the population multiplied fast occupying a wide variety of environment in Australia from sub-alpine to subtropical zones and towards middle of the 19th century there were several hundred million rabbits and had attained the status of serious pest population. The search of natural enemies for rabbit was made and found that myxoma virus could multiply as an epizoite on rabbits and that mosquitoes could be natural vectors for the mechanical transfer of the parasite. The virus causes serious disease, myxomatosis in rabbits leading to high mortality rate in animal.

The action of natural selection on two different species occupying different tropich levels can be regarded as an excellent model for the co-evolutionary process seem to occur between host and its new parasite. The parasite maximise its chances of survival, successfully live on the host and do little damage to it. Host survival depends on its ability to resist the effect of the parasite. Natural selection favours the parasites that can maintain their infectivity and host can become resistance to infections or toxic effects of the parasite once the infection has occurred.

Q4. Industrial melanism is an excellent model to demonstrate the natural selection in action. Analyse the above statement critically.

Ans. Melanism occurs in many species, and has recently become a useful trait for understanding how selection acts on genes. Here we discuss melanism in peppered moths. A moth species had two color forms, black and white. The industrial revolution caused most things in urban environments to become coated with black ash, including the trunks of trees. Insect collectors noticed they found only the black form of the moth on the bark. They assumed all the white moths had been eaten by birds, because they now were highly visible against the black background. This meant black (melanistic) moths were better adapted to survive and had replaced the white variety. They were found resting on light coloured and lichen encrusted trees. Careful searching eventually revealed the white moths had simply begun congregating on any white objects they could find. The population was just the same as before the sooty smoke. The error in the initial assumption was the moths were unable to make decisions based on observations of their environment. Most 19th century Victorians assumed non-human animals were just mindless robots, especially simple forms such as insects.

Industrial melanism was observed by H.B.D. Kettlewell and E.B. Ford who studied the phenomenon in found that a single dominant gene for melanism is present in moth, *Biston betularia*. The frequency of gene increased from less than 1% in pre-industrial times to more than 90% with the onset of industrial revolution in less than fifty generations of the insect. As seen in the table below:

Table 12.1

		Typical Form	**Carboniria**
Unpolluted Woodland	Released	496	473
	Recaptured	62 (12.5%)	30(6.3%)
Soot-polluted Woodland	Released	137	447
	Recaptured	34(16%)	154(34%)

Q5. What do you understand by sexual selection. Illustrate your answer with a suitable example.

Ans. Charles Darwin distinguished sexual selection as variance in the number of mates. Sexual selection acts to refine secondary sexual characters of the phenotype such as morphological differences between males and females, or differences between male types. Primary sexual characters are the basic differences between male and female reproductive genital systems. The action of sexual selection can take the same three modes that are discussed above for natural selection.

The competition for mates has resulted in the selection of certain secondary sexual characters. In males there is a constant evolution of such characters which are attractive to female counterparts like brilliant colours, elaborate comb, bright plumage, extensive horns, ornamental tusks and aggressive behaviour are all secondary sexual characters evolved by males to attract females. Sexual selection can be regarded as competition among the members to win the opposite sex.

The sexual selection is more pronounced in polygamous societies. Examples of sexual selection are the mating behaviour of fur seal, *Callorhinus ursinus* in Pribilof island near Alaska. The males of fur seal are one-and-a-half time longer and six time as heavy as females. Prior to mating the sea bulls meet in the breeding ground and engage in a fierce battle. Many males die in the encounter and other run away from the scene. The victo eventually settle down on the rockey shore with harem of cows. In African widow bird, there is marked sexual dimorphism, in male birds there is half a meter long showy tail and prominent patches on the wings whereas females have short tail and are dull coloured. Anderson by cutting the tail of male made three classes of birds with short tails, normal tails and long tails. When these birds released into their natural habitat, they were able to establish their own territories and birds with short tails were least successful in attracting females than the one with long tail. This shows that certain characters play an important role in maintaining the differences between the sexes and the female's choice confers n adaptive advantage on the males.

Q6. How would you answer the criticism against Darwinism that common altruistic behaviour of individuals provided evidence contrary to the theory of natural selection?

Ans. The behaviour pattern of an individual in a population for the benefit of other members is refered as altruism where gene for altruism regulates the behaviour of such individuals. Such individuals exhibiting altruistic behaviour may or may not survive. For example bird giving warning signal in order to alert other individuals may itself invite the attention of predator and die and death of such a bird may also result the eliminations of concerned genes for such behaviour. Altruism as a behaviour pattern is an adaptation and such individuals are victims of this behaviour. This shows that genes considered to be adaptive or favourable ones are eliminated, although natural selection is supposed to promote such favourable genes in the population.

W. D. Hamilton proposed the term **kin selection** to explain the altruistic behaviour. For instance mother expending energy suckling or caring for her children and ensure only reproductive success of her own genes through her progeny. Kin selection favours such behaviour when the risk taken or energy spent by individual is more than compensated by the benefits accrued by the relatives. Another example is that a parent has more than two offspring and assumes that parents meet an altruistic death while defending its children. Here the selection would promote gene for parental altruism through progeny. J. B. S. Haldane explains altruism and kin selection by statement "I will lay down my life for two of my brothers or eight of my cousins". The probability of one's genes shared by his brothers or sisters is one half and that of cousins is one's eighth.

If individuals were to die because of altruistic behaviour, there are greater chances for his genes to spread in the population through his sibs or cousins. But if individual remain selfish, not only his own life may lost but of relative as well. For instance a warning call not given at the sight of predator or intruder may possibly wipe out the entire genome of population. The best example of this behaviour is seen in honey bee consists of a queen, several haploid drones and large number of diploid females. Nearly 75% of genome of workers is common and do variety of job whereas drone and queen concerned with reproduction. They are altruistic in real sense. Being sterile, they have no chance of spreading their genes in population directly and ensure with the altruistic behaviour that colony continue and have greater probability of spreading their genes in the population directly. They raise one of their sisters to the status of queen. The natural selection explains the existence of sterile female workers in a beehive.

Q7. With the help of suitable example explain the co-evolution of prey-predators.

Ans. The process by which one organism as predator eats other organism as prey is called as predation. If the prey population becomes abundant the predator population also become abundant and if predator is abundant and efficient, there will be reduction in the abundance of the prey population. Prey-predator relationships can be visualised as a game where each player outwit the other and individuals better adapted to escape predation would survive and reproduce. So in prey-predators with varying degrees of efficiency, the prey species evolves towards maintaining predation and making more efficient. Such a coevolution of the predator-prey relationship may continue indefinitely over long periods without causing extinction of both species. This is achieved by improving the efficiency of the predator and the resistance of the prey in a balanced way. Natural selection aims at faster improvement of the efficiency of an inefficient predator than the resistance in an already resistant prey.

Example among the predators are: the long and slimy tongue and accurate aim of insectivorous lizards; the elaborate webs of spiders; hunting behaviour of lion cryptic colouration, fleetness, noxious substances and toxins, alarm calls and posting of sentinels can be cited as instances of adaptations evolved by prey organism as defensive measures.

Q8. Distinguish between group selection and kin selection.

Ans. In general **group selection** refers to the idea that certain genes survive because they are good for the group though not necessarily for individuals (e.g. altruistic or self-sacrificing genes). The individual may not survive, but the group will.

Group selection refers to the idea that alleles can become fixed or spread in a population because of the benefits they bestow on groups, regardless of the fitness of individuals within that group.

The effect of natural selection on colonies or population favouring one group as preference to other. The fitness of genotypes between groups may vary within population and on other hand consider a colony of individuals with gene restricting population growth, optimum use of food resources of the environment. The selection would essentially favour the latter group and the former may eventually face extinction.

Kin selection refers only to those acts or traits that increase the fitness of relatives (and therefore one's owns through relatives). It is a subcategory of group selection, where the group is formed of related organisms.

Kin selection refers to changes in gene frequency across generations that are driven at least in part by interactions between related individuals.

The term kin selection can be equated to natural selection when we consider kin or relative of an individual. For example mother expanding energy suckling or taking care of children and ensures reproductive success of her own genes through her progeny. Being sterile they have no chance to spread their genes in the population directly but by their altruistic behaviour they ensure the continuance of colony and have greater probability of spreading their genes in the colony while raising one of their sisters to the status of queen as seen in the bees.

Q9. Describe the co-evolution of plants and herbivores in the plant- herbivore system.

Ans. Co-evolution between plants and herbivorous animals has been developed into mutually beneficial relationship. Plants are good source of food for animals like insects, birds and mammals and in return help plants in dispersal of pollen and seeds. Plants offer insects both nectar and pollen as food anf\d insects in turn have developed olfactory, isual and structural adaptations for pollination and dispersal. Many animals help plants in return for food they get from them by dispersing their seeds to faraway places. Plants have evolved colourful, fleshy and nutritious fruits and on being eaten and defecated by birds in environments favourable to the plants and seeds germinate and grow. Large herbivores like elephants, rhinos and giraffes consume fruits and help in dispersal. It has been found that in Central America a large number of herbivores like camels, horses, giant armadillos, elephants etc. were responsible for the dispersal of trees and shrubs during Pleistocene times but with the extinction of these animals some 10,000 years ago, the trees also disappeared and only remnants survive today.

Besides such adaptations which promote mutualism, plants have evolved adaptations to protect themselves from the attack of herbivores which is one of the co-evolutionary process. Plants tend to develop adaptations to protect them from herbivores feed on them. Some plants store toxic substance in their tissues to protect them from potential eaters. Some plants have anti-juvenile hormone which is a terpenoid found in insects being secreted by an endocrine gland the corpus allatum and it regulates the metamorphosis of insects. The insects feeding on such plants have their corpus allatum switched off by the precocenes as they are capableto enter in blood and can make insect die without reproducing.

Another example of monarch butterfly being despised by blue jays feed on milkweed plants accumulates cardiac glycosides and experience severe vomiting provoked by the chemical. The grasshopper which is not predated by birds and insects feed on another member of family Aselepediaceae do accumulate cardiac glycosides.

CHAPTER-13

SPECIATION

INTRODUCTION

Speciation is important in evolution as it leads to progressive evolution and diversity in nature. Ernst Mayr studied species and its problems and points out that speciation, the multiplication of species i.e. Division of one parent species into several daughter species is the process responsible for the evolutionary diversity of organic world. Darwin in his book ' Origin of Species defined the word species precisely although he interpreted speciation in terms of reproductive isolation and emphasised that occupation of an unique ecological niche by each species could be a major characteristic of speciation. The concepts related to speciation has been discussed.

Q1. Briefly comment on three types of species concept.

Or

Write a short note on Biological concept of speciation.

[Dec-2019, Q.No.-6 (b)]

Ans. Species have been offered many definitions but none of them proved to be satisfactory as it did not provide basis to decide whether two similar groups are distinct species or only sub-species.

Three types of species concept have been proposed specifically as:

- **Typological Species Concept:** This was suggested by Plato more than 2000 years ago and according to this concept, the immense variety in nature can be reduced to a few types. Individuals may vary but they belong to a single type. It is just a morphological species concept as most modern evolutionist found the typological species inadequate as it is static and fails to capture the dynamism of speciation as evolutionary process.

- **Nominalistic Species Concept:** The nominalists deny the existence of Plato's 'Types' as for them only individual exists and species are man-made artificial abstraction. Biologists who studied plants and animals in their natural conditions have observed closely and claim that this concept is not true.

- **Biological Species Concept:** This concept consists of natural population and species are real and objective and not man-made subjective abstraction. In this concept, the members of species are reproductive community and species is an ecological unit, it interacts with other species and shares the resources of the environment and are in gene pool and the concept has been confirmed by Harvard evolutionist, Ernst Mayr. According to Mayr," Species are groups of interbreeding natural populations that are reproductively isolated from other such groups". The biological species is not only a distinct unit at any given time but also has the evolutionary capacity to change continuously over long periods of time, measured in millions of years.

Q2. Distinguish the terms sympatric, peripatric and allopatric speciation.

Ans. Three different types of speciation was recognised by the biologist.

- **Sympatric speciation:** In this type of speciation, the parent species gives rise to a daughter species without the individuals of a species being separated by space or territory. Both instantaneous and gradual models of sympatric speciation have been proposed barring one mode of instantaneous speciation by a mechanism known as polyploidy whereas other modes of sympatric speciation remained controversial.

  It has been found that sympatric speciation may occur whenever disruptive or diversifying selection is active. For example, take a population of individuals with genotypes AA and A'A', each of which is adapted to live specifically on plant species 1 and 2 respectively. The heterozygote AA' is not well adapted to either species of plants, that means homozygote would have higher fitness if it mated assortatively or non-random mating i.e. males and females of similar genotypes tend to mate each other. Such an assertive mating minimize the production of unfit heterozygous progeny and selection process would tend to establish two different populations of distinct genotype.

  Another locus B may be conferring the assortative mating trait on two genotypes and this influence the mating behaviour and impel organism to choose the specific host species for mating and laying eggs. The genotypes BB and bb may mate and lay eggs on host 1 and bb on host 2. This difference results in the selection of specific host and isolates the two genotypes reproductively. In phytophygous insects such as treehoppers, closely related species are confined to different host plants for feeding and breeding.

- **Allopatric speciation:** The most common mode of species formation among animals, speciation by population of parent species occupies separate territories occurs in large areas in the vast continental slopes and ocean floors. The population is divided into two newly formed barrier may be a desert, river or mountain range. The population on other side of new barrier becomes geographically isolated. The separation may be gradual and the model is called as **dumbbell model** as shown in the figure below:

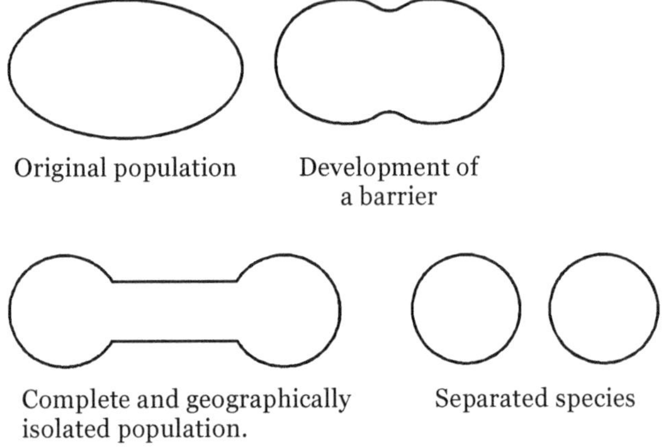

Fig. 13.1

The speciation occurs in allopatric system by more or less equal subdivision of large population. This speciation is a characteristic of K strategists which are highly mobile, long lived and high in competitive ability.

- **Peripatric Speciation:** The small population isolated on the periphery of the distribution of the parent population can be described as peripaytric speciation. The small, peripheral populations occupy ecological niches not occupied by parental population and the founder populations can carry only a small part of the genetic variabilityof the parent population.

As explained in the Figure below, initially species consists of uniformly distributed individuals grouped as populations between which there is limited gene flow which keeps the population as an integrated species. As long as there free flow of genes, even if it were to be limited, a new species cannot be formed.

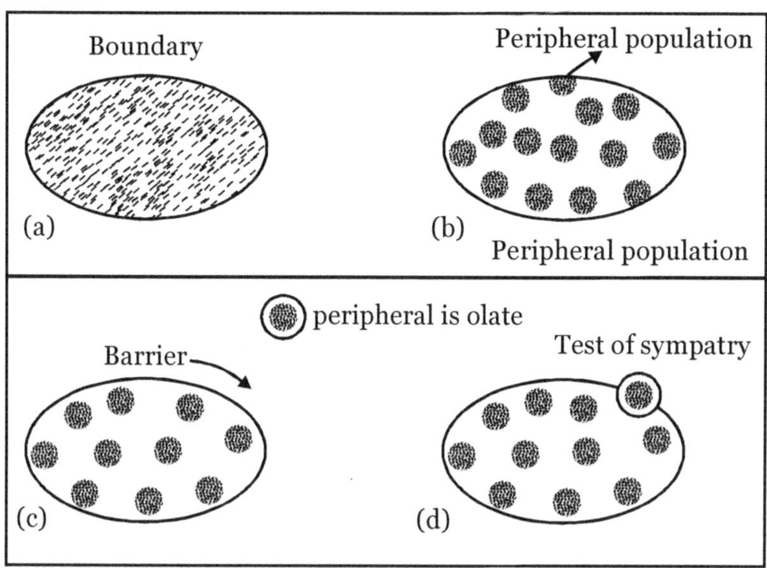

Fig. 13.2

The individuals living in the periphery of a population may experience less gene flow than central population but they still form an integral part of species. Only when the population is a peripheral isolate and not just a peripheral population, it has a possibility of becoming a new species as shown in the figure.

Q3. What do you understand by the term ring species? Illustrate your answer with suitable example.

Ans. In the concept of speciation, a widely used species break up into partially rule species and different subspecies are further differentiated due to action of selection and other factors. This forms a circle or group of races or **Rassenkreis** and the terminal members of such a circle will sufficiently different from others so that a sterility barrier sets in.

To understand the concept let us consider an example of two high mountains in west coast of USA, the ranges are Coastal range and Sierra Nevada. At their northern ends near Canadian border they are united as shown in the figure. Towards south they are separated by hot and arid desert. Further south, close to Mexican border, these mountains meet again. There is an amphibian species, *Ensatina eschscholtzii* at the place A as marked in figure. It is supposed that this original species split into two populations B and G which moved down the two respective mountain ranges. On one range the population change gradually from B to C to D to E and on to F. On the other mountain range the population G, like B derived from A gradually moved south changing into H, I, J and K. While these changing were taking place, the two series were isolated from each other by a desert. Since the *Ensatina* has poor locomotor power, it must have taken thousands of years to proceed to Canadian boarder. This shows that population B and G will have the least amount of isolating mechanisms where D and I have more and greater between E and I. Both BCDE and GHIJ series are derived from single species *Ensatina eschscholtzii* designated as A. On reaching the Mexican border, the two populations F and K are able to overlap without mating as seen in the figure. They have passed the test of sympatry and F and K are now two distinct species. Similar ring species have been shown to occur in sea-gulls forming a **circumpolar ring** around the world.

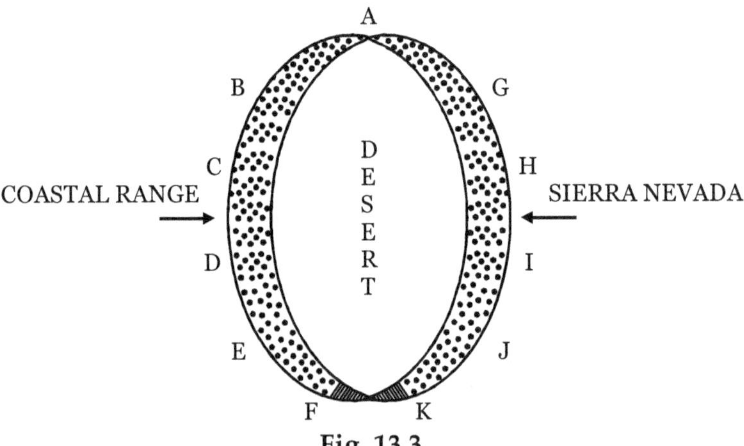

Fig. 13.3

Q4. What do you mean by isolating mechanism in the species? What is the difference between pre- and post- mating isolating mechanisms?

Ans. Isolating mechanisms are intrinsic characteristics of species that reduce or prevent successful reproduction with members of other species. Viewed genetically, they are characters that act as barriers to the exchange of genes between populations. Most of these barriers are incidental consequences of divergence between populations but they can be elaborated by natural selection. They can take many forms, from mismatches between mating signals and preferences to genetic incompatibilities causing sterility of hybrids. A major outstanding challenge is to document the contributions of different forms of isolation to the overall barrier to gene exchange between species and to understand the order in which these barriers evolve.

The reproductive characteristics, which prevent species from fusing: Isolating mechanisms are particularly important in the *biological species concept,* in which species of sexual organisms are defined by *reproductive isolation,* i.e. a lack of gene mixture. Two broad kinds of isolating mechanisms between species are typically distinguished, together with a number of sub-types:

(1) Pre-mating isolating mechanisms: Factors which cause species to mate with their own kind (*assortative mating*).

(i) *Temporal isolation:* Individuals of different species do not mate because they are active at different times of day or in different seasons.

(ii) **Ecological isolation:** Individuals mate in their preferred habitat, and therefore do not meet individuals of other species with different ecological preferences.

(iii) **Behavioral isolation:** Potential mates meet, but choose members of their own species.

(iv) **Mechanical isolation:** Copulation is attempted, but transfer of sperm does not take place.

(2) Post-mating isolating mechanisms: Genomic incompatibility, hybrid inviability or sterility.

(i)   Gametic incompatibility: Sperm transfer takes place, but egg is not fertilized.

(ii) Zygotic mortality: Egg is fertilized, but zygote does not develop.

(iii) Hybrid inviability: Hybrid embryo forms, but of reduced viability.

(iv) Hybrid sterility: Hybrid is viable, but resulting adult is sterile.

(v)   Hybrid breakdown: First generation (F1) hybrids are viable and fertile, but further hybrid generations (F2 and backcrosses) may be inviable or sterile.

An alternative classification of isolating mechanisms contrasts pre-zygotic isolation (items 1+ 2a above) with post-zygotic isolation (items 2b-e above). As an example of the application of isolating mechanisms, the apple-feeding host race of the tephritid fruit fly (Rhagoletis pomonella) differs from the hawthorn-feeding race in that the apple race emerges earlier in the year (1a), and each host race preferentially chooses to rest, lay eggs and mate on its own host plant (1b). On the other hand, laboratory experiments show that there is little behavioral, mechanical, or post-mating isolation.

The term isolating mechanisms was introduced by T Dobzhansky in the 1930s, and has been popularized by E Mayr. Both originally proposed that isolating mechanisms were group traits beneficial at the level of the species; today, this is generally disbelieved. Recent biologists have pointed out that the word "mechanism" is particularly misleading as pre-mating and post-mating isolation are likely to evolve as a by-product of natural selection or genetic drift within species, rather than as a direct result of their utility as barriers to fertilization and gene mixing between species (a process known as reinforcement). A leading critic of the biological species concept and of the term isolating mechanisms is HEH Paterson, who argues that species are cohesive and as a result of pre-zygotic sexual signaling within species, rather than due to isolating mechanisms between species. Paterson therefore introduced a competing idea of species, the recognition concept of species, in which isolating mechanisms were replaced by specific mate recognition systems as an alternative. Unfortunately, the word "system" has as many group-benefit connotations as "mechanism", and the recognition concept of species has not gained universal acceptance.

There is also the terminological problem that reproductive isolation combines traits that reduce gene flow, such as mate choice or fertilization barriers, with traits that select against genes that have flowed, such as hybrid incompatibility. Lumping these two antagonistic features is confusing, since they are unrelated and evolve in very different ways. For instance, whereas it is conceivable that reinforcement might evolve to reduce an individual's tendency to mate with another species and produce inviable offspring, it is almost impossible to imagine that hybrid inviability itself would evolve as an adaptation. This reproductive isolation terminology leads also to a muddled use of the term gene flow as the opposite of reproductive isolation; in other words, gene flow comes to include not only the flow of genes, but also the effects of any natural selection on the frequency of such genes within each population.

The most fundamental problem with isolating mechanisms (and specific mate recognition systems) is that species are implied to be qualitatively different from subspecies, races, or forms by their possession of these traits. Races cannot, in theory, differ in either type of trait because only species are defined by their possession. Arguably, by making species seem qualitatively different from races, these terms have spawned a number of special models of speciation where **geographic isolation,** also known as allopatry, or sudden bursts of evolution in small founder populations (founder events or punctuated equilibria) play important roles. Only such unusual conditions were thought to be able to give rise to new species that differ in isolating mechanisms (or specific mate recognition systems). In reality, there is little to distinguish mate choice and disruptive natural selection commonly observed within species from pre-mating and post-mating isolation between species; and, indeed, it is hard to distinguish species from races in many actual organisms (see **species concepts**).

Most serious research on speciation now avoids using the term isolating mechanisms because of these unwanted connotations. Instead, researchers clearly distinguish between mate choice, hybrid incompatibility and other forms of reproductive isolation.

Q5. What is genetic drift?

Ans. The genetic drift is a process that may operate in small populations bringing about large scale changes in gene frequencies. Genetic drift describes random fluctuations in the numbers of gene variants in a population. Genetic drift takes place when the occurrence of variant forms of a gene, called alleles, increases and decreases by chance over time. These variations in the presence of alleles are measured as changes in allele frequencies. It is also known as **Sewall Wright effect.**

Typically, genetic drift occurs in small populations, where infrequently occurring alleles face a greater chance of being lost. Once it begins, genetic drift will continue until the involved allele is either lost by a population or until it is the only allele present in a population at a particular locus. Both possibilities decrease the genetic diversity of a population. Genetic drift is common after population bottlenecks, which are events that drastically decrease the size of a population. In these cases, genetic drift can result in the loss of rare alleles and decrease the gene pool. Genetic drift can cause a new population to be genetically distinct from its original population, which has led to the hypothesis that genetic drift plays a role in the evolution of new species.

Q6. In small populations the gene frequencies often tend to drift. Justify the logic of the statement with suitable example.

Ans. It has been observed that in small populations genetic drift occurs due to sampling error. It refers to accidental but pronounced fluctuations in the frequency of a particular allele. In a population consisting of 100 individuals, assuming an allele in present only in one individual, the chances are that either the allele is irrevocably eliminated from the population in one or two generations on the frequency of allele may increase by 10%. The genes may be consequently lost or completely fixed in small populations.

Genetic drift can be demonstrated by small experiment. Let us take beads of same size having different colours say blue, red, green and yellow. Take thousands of different colours beads in a bag. The 4000 beads constitute the population. Now take out 4 beads without looking from the bag. Let us say we got two blue, one red and one green. This means blues have increased from 25-50% but yellows are reduced to zero. This experiment shows that random drifting or large scale changes in frequency of colour beads are a result of sampling error. The frequency of coloured beads drift randomly in the experiment in small population or peripheral isolates gene frequencies may drift due to sampling error and the phenomenon is known as genetic drift.

Q7. With the help of a suitable example explain how " habitat preferences of an organism promotes speciation".

Ans. Ecological isolation is based on the fact that population shows preference to one habitat over the other. Differences in breeding dates and occupation of different habitats outside breeding season are the contributing factors for the minimum competition and niche overlap among the species. There are instances where potential mates keep away from each other because of their habitat preferences. In these cases there might even be a broad niche overlap and the individuals may exist in the same area but the distinctness of sub-species and species is maintained. The example from united states where the two sub-species of mice, *Peromyscus maniculatus* have overlapping niches and do not interbreed in nature although interbreeding is observed in the laboratory. In other example of water snake, *Natrix sipedon* may come close together but may not interbreed because of their habitat preferences.

CHAPTER-14

HUMAN EVOLUTION-I

INTRODUCTION

Human evolution is the lengthy process of change by which people originated from apelike ancestors. Scientific evidence shows that the physical and behavioral traits shared by all people originated from apelike ancestors and evolved over a period of approximately six million years.

Humans are primates. Physical and genetic similarities show that the modern humanspecies, Homo sapiens, has a very close relationship to another group of primate species, the apes. Humans and the great apes (large apes) of Africa -- chimpanzees (including bonobos, or so-called "pygmy chimpanzees") and gorillas -- share a common ancestor that lived between 8 and 6 million years ago. Humans first evolved in Africa, and much of human evolution occurred on that continent. The fossils of early humans who lived between 6 and 2 million years ago come entirely from Africa.

There is little fossil evidence for the divergence of the gorilla, chimpanzee and hominin lineages. The earliest fossils that have been proposed as members of the hominin lineage are Sahelanthropus tchadensis dating from 7 million years ago, Orrorin tugenensis dating from 5.7 million years ago, and Ardipithecus kadabba dating to 5.6 million years ago. Each of these have been argued to be a bipedalancestor of later hominins but, in each case, the claims have been contested.

Q1. Write briefly on the primate lineage of hominid ancestory.

Ans. The primate family hominidae consists of two commonly accepted genera, Australopithecus and Homo. However, two other genera are proposed. The genus <u>Ardipithecus</u> has recently been described and placed as the earliest common ancestor to all hominids.

When considering human origins it is important to keep in mind the nature and structure of the primate evolutionary tree. Primates are the product of significant mammalian adaptive radiations which occurred throughout the early Tertiary, ~ 70–50 mya (millions of years ago). Within the development of extant (living) primates, there have also been several adaptive radiations (~ 50 mya-present). The emergence of hominids came from a common ancestor of extant apes and humans from approximately 6–7 mya. Modern apes, (chimpanzees), are not our immediate ancestors or progenitors but rather more appropriately, our siblings. Both exist in the temporal present and have only morphologically distinct parent taxa to serve as a common ancestor. According to this view, the australopithecines, like the ardipithecines, are hominid radiations. One species-level taxa from the ardipithecies gave rise to the australopithecine radiation. Likewise, from this radiation came one Australopithecus species that gave rise to the Homo lineage.

The latter family includes species such as *H. habilis*, *H. erectus* and *H. sapiens*. The relationship between the three commonly accepted species of Homo is subject to some controversy as recent analyses have concluded australopithecine affinities of *H. habilis*.

Some view the emergence of *H. erectus* as the hallmark of the modern human race. This view is attractive for those wishing to argue regional continuity of H. erectus in Eurasia with modern human populations. This regional approach posits that the various species of hominids out of Africa are members of the same lineage, only separated by time.

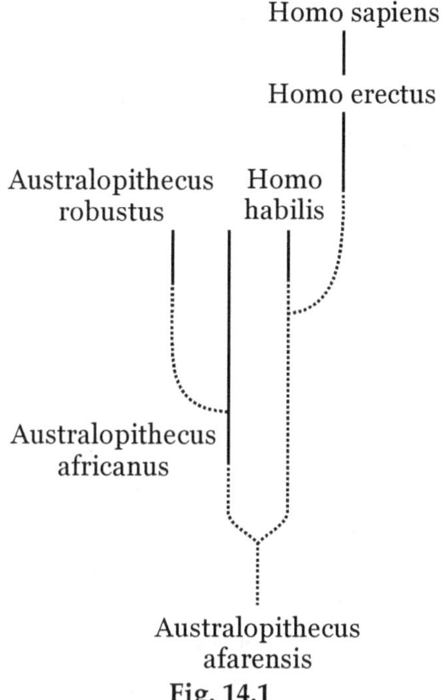

Fig. 14.1

Q2. How would you justify that australopithecines were human ancestors?

Ans. Raymond Dart (1925) was the first to describe an australopithecine in the literature when he published a description of the now famous Taung Child discovered in South Africa the previous year. This individual was a juvenile specimen attributed to the species *Australopithecus africanus*. The name Australopithecus translates to 'southern ape'. This nomenclature can largely be attributed to the ape-like features of the cranium and the location of its discovery (a Limestone cave in South Africa). However, since this time, the genus has been discovered in the eastern part of Africa as well. The defining features of the australopithecines as a clade can be summarized as follows (White 2002). It should be noted that these defining characteristics apply to both the 'gracile' (Australopithecus) and 'robust' (Paranthropus) varieties.

- Anatomy adapted to bipedal locomotion

- High brachial index (forearm/upper arm ratio) relative to other hominids
- Sexually dimorphic to a degree greater than Homo and Pan, but less than Gorilla or Pongo
- Height: 1.2 m – 1.5 m; Mass: 30 kg – 55 kg (estimated)
- Cranial capacity: 350 cc – 600 cc
- Postcanine dentition relatively large, enamel thickened compared to contemporary apes and humans
- Incisors and canine relatively small, little sexual dimorphism in canines compared to modern apes

The adaptation to bipedal locomotion (1) is of particular significance in human evolution. All australopithecines possess anatomical characteristics of the pelvis, femur and spinal column that facilitate bipedal locomotion. Whether or not the australopithecines were fully adapted bipeds is still hotly debated in the literature. There is lot of evidence to suggest a hominid ancestory in australopithecines. They had developed upright walking and an increased cranial capacity relative to their primate ancestors. They had a cave dwelling habit and there is evidence to suggest that they made stone tools and developed a social life.

Q3. Make a comparison of the characters of *Homo erectus* and *Homo sapiens* based on fossil evidence.

Or

Discuss the major trends in evolution of hte genus Honosapiens.

[Dec-2019, Q.No.-4 (a)]

Ans. Homo Erectus: *Homo erectus* was one of the hominid species, which is now extinct from the world. They were the first to stand in a standard upright posture out of all the hominids, and that has given their species name *erectus*. According to the fossil evidences, they lived until 1.3 million years from today and the earliest Homo erectus fossil dates back to 1.8 million years. Until recent findings about the fossils of *Homo habilis*, it was believed that *H. erectus* descended into *H. neanderthalensis*. However, now the scientists state that both these species lived together for at least 500,000 years. *H. erectus* was the first to move out from Africa, and they have gone into many places of the world as their fossils from different regions of the world suggest. They were highly intelligent creatures, and it is envisaged as some had cranial capacities differing between 850 and 1,100 cubic centimetres. The face profile was not much protruded like in Australopithecus, and erectus man was averagely 5 feet and 10 inches tall. Additionally, the females were considerably smaller than males (by 25%). There are evidences to suggest that they used fire and tools in easing their functions. Furthermore, they have used rafts to cross water bodies that measure up to even oceans.

Homo Sapiens: It is the scientifically referred name for the modern man, and the two names together means the man who thinks or the wise man. The human is one of the most distinguished species of the entire animal kingdom. They perform highly complex activities and solve serious matters or problems using the exceptionally large brain compared to the body size. It has been a widely accepted fact that the human's primary weapon is the brain, or in other words, the intelligence of man could never be beaten by any of the forces in the universe. The highly complex and developed brain of the humans has the ability to theorize languages, justifications, problem solving, and many more functions. Humans are distributed all over the world including the ice-cold snowed lands all around the year, but not in Antarctica. They are culturally different among nations as well as within nations and countries. Mainly, there are three morphological types of humans known as Mongoloid, Caucasoid, and Negroid. However, the number of differences among human individuals is countless, because all the human individuals are extremely different from each other in their external appearance as well as from their thoughts. Nevertheless, the physiology has no much difference from the related species. Usually a healthy average adult human weighs about 50 – 80 kilograms while the height could vary from 1.5 to 1.8 metres. Despite the fact that humans are the most sophisticated species ever known to live on the Earth, the ability to stand out any major disaster or a climatic or geographic shift is unknown, but other animals have proven their abilities in such occasions.

Main points of difference between Homo sapiens and Homo erectus:

- ***H. sapiens*** is a presently surviving or thriving species while ***H. erectus*** was a prehistoric and extinct species.
- The cranial capacity is higher in the modern man compared to *H. erectus*.
- The face profile of the *H. sapiens* is not as protruded as in *H. erectus*.
- The skin of the *H. erectus* would have had more hair cover than in the humans.
- *Homo sapiens* is the human, whereas *H. erectus* was a human-like or hominid species.
- The average height was slightly higher in *H.erectus* as compared to humans.
- The sexual dimorphism was more pronounced in *H. erectus* man than in the modern man.

Q4. Briefly comment on the possible hominid phylogeny.

Ans. Recent discoveries of new fossil hominid species have been accompanied by several phylogenetic hypotheses. All of these hypotheses are based on a consideration of hominid craniodental morphology. The hominid family had its origin from the Dryopithecine ancestors. Fossil record suggests that Proconsul and Ramapithecus is quite near to family Hominidae. However, Collard and Wood (2000) suggested that cladograms derived from craniodental data are inconsistent with the prevailing hypothesis of ape phylogeny based on molecular data. The implication of their study is that craniodental characters are unreliable indicators of phylogeny in hominoids and fossil hominids but, notably, their analysis did not include extinct species. The cladistic analysis designed to test whether the inclusion of fossil taxa affects the ability of morphological characters to recover the molecular ape phylogeny. One hundred and ninety-eight craniodental characters were examined, including 109 traits that traditionally have been of interest in prior studies of hominoid and early hominid phylogeny, and 89 craniometric traits that represent size-corrected linear dimensions measured between standard cranial landmarks. The characters were partitioned into two data sets. One set contained all of the characters, and the other omitted the craniometric characters. Six parsimony analyses were performed; each data set was analyzed three times, once using an ingroup that consisted only of extant hominoids, a second time using an ingroup of extant hominoids and extinct early hominids, and a third time excluding Kenyanthropus platyops.

Results suggest that the inclusion of fossil taxa can play a significant role in phylogenetic analysis. Analyses that examined only extant taxa produced most parsimonious cladograms that were inconsistent with the ape molecular tree.

In contrast, analyses that included fossil hominids were consistent with that tree. This consistency refutes the basis for the hypothesis that craniodental characters are unreliable for reconstructing phylogenetic relationships. Regarding early hominids, the relationships of *Sahelanthropus tchadensis* and *Ardipithecus ramidus* were relatively unstable.

However, there is tentative support for the hypotheses that *S. tchadensis* is the sister taxon of all other hominids. There is support for the hypothesis that *A. anamensis* is the sister taxon of all hominids except *S. tchadensis* and *Ar. ramidus*.

There is no compelling support for the hypothesis that *Kenyanthropus platyops* shares especially close affinities with *Homo rudolfensis*. Rather, K. platyops is nested within the Homo + Paranthropus + *Australopithecus africanus* clade. If K. *platyops* is a valid species, these relationships suggest that *Homo* and *Paranthropus* are likely to have diverged from other hominids much earlier than previously supposed.

There is no support for the hypothesis that A. garhi is either the sister taxon or direct ancestor of the genus Homo. Phylogenetic relationships indicate that Australopithecus is paraphyletic. Thus, *A. anamensis* and *A. garhi* should be allocated to new genera. *Australopithecus afarensis* was discovered during pliocene period as hominoid fossil and the genus Homo is derived from australopithecine species.

The main aim of GPH book is to provide knowledge as well as good marks in exam.

CHAPTER-15

HUMAN EVOLUTION-II

INTRODUCTION

Today modern man is regarded as climax of the evolutionary process. The chapter deals with cultural evolution of man. The most important aspect of cultural evolution in humans is communication skills and language development. Present study deals with families and societies and also discuss whether natural selection is still active on present day man and the trends in future evolution of man.

Q1. Do you think that ability to express has distinguished man from other animal groups and made him superior to them? Briefly substantiate your claim.

Ans. What makes a man different from other animal is his ability to form connections and it usually begins with the curiosity with how and why things work and what will be the outcome if we were to alter things to better orient ourselves in the world. Our ability to understand abstract thought and concepts, and our ability to use language to explain our thoughts and reasoning, our self awareness and the understanding that we are conscious and self aware entities. Man more than any species try to convey uniqueness to our own image, character, temperament and personality. Because of our self awareness is more than positive.

There are two opinions regarding the superiority of human species in terms of their ability to express better than animals. Dobzhansky and Simpson are of the view that language makes a man superior to other animals. Other view is that there is indeed a continuity in morphology of apes and mankind and this continuity is recognised in language, self-awareness and other facilities as well.

Q2. How is the tool making ability linked with the development of communication abilities in humans?

Ans. Human language and human conversation might have originated as a way to help our ancestors teach each other tool-making skills, a crucial ability in our evolution. Exactly when humans began talking amongst themselves has long been a subject of debate, with estimations ranging from as recently as 50,000 years ago to all the way back to human origins 2 million years in the past.

Spoken words are incapable of leaving any trace in the physical archaeological record – writing and written evidence would come much later, so previous studies have concentrated on other indicators, such as early cave art or tool making skills, that might serve as similar evidence of symbolic abilities in humans.

However, such evidence has been seen as lacking sufficient evidence to settle the debate on when language first evolved. Instead of looking at tool making as possible proxy evidence of language use, researchers decided to see if language could help modern humans make ancient tools, known as Oldowan tools after the area in Tanzania where they were first uncovered.

There is correlation between tool making ability and development of communication skills. The movement of tongue and mouth are commonly associated with hard work. Hand gestures appear to have predated spoken language as a form of communication and involve sequential elaboration of their component parts and have to be developed in a specific order. Symbolic and spoken languages often come to be written and advantage here is that if forgotten, it can be retrieved again. This methodology improves the content of any culture and promotes accuracy. With the explosion in knowledge, it became difficult to transmute, condense and generate knowledge in the minds of men and hence, books came into being. The creation of knowledge is a collective task and is not dependent on single person. Writing play significant role in the cultural evolution of man and accessibility of books to all people was responsible for the spread of knowledge.

Q3. Is evolution of culture distinct from biological evolution of man? Justify your answer.

Ans. After some three billion years, the Darwinian era is over. The epoch of species competition came to an end about 10 thousand years ago when a single species, Homo sapiens, began to dominate and reorganize the planet. Since that time, cultural evolution has replaced biological evolution as the driving force of change. The culture it appears is not transmitted by genes and therefore superorganic. The fact remains that it is only the possessors of human genotype who can acquire, transmit, innovative or transmute culture. The cultural evolution could be potentially self-destructive if the adaptation is to culture itself and not to the external environment. To distinguish cultural evolution from biological evolution it is said that man may adapt expanding automobile culture but at the same time he should also evolve the biological adaptations and ability to withstand pollution. So we can say that there is definite advantage by replacing the biological evolution with cultural one leads to faster change.

Biological evolution is a slow and tedious process as compared to cultural evolution and the difference in two processes allow man to adjust to environmental changes. It is said that culture has very subtly delinked the genome of man from his geophysical environment.

Q4. Do you believe that natural selection plays relatively a lesser role in evolving adaptation in man as compared to other groups of organisms?

Ans. Natural selection is the gradual process by which heritable biological traits become either more or less common in a population as a function of the effect of inherited traits on the differential reproductive success of organisms interacting with their environment. The term "natural selection" was given by Charles Darwin, who intended it to be compared with artificial selection, now more commonly referred to as selective breeding.

Variation exists within all populations of organisms. This occurs partly because random mutations arise in the genome of an individual organism, and these mutations can be passed to offspring. Throughout the individuals' lives, their genomes interact with their environments to cause variations in traits. The environment of a genome includes the molecular biology in the cell, other cells, other individuals, populations, species, as well as the abiotic environment. Individuals with certain variants of the trait may survive and reproduce more than individuals with other, less successful, variants. Therefore the population evolves. Factors that affect reproductive success are also important, an issue that Charles Darwin developed in his ideas on sexual selection and fecundity selection,

Natural selection directs genetic changes when adapted to the environment are retained in the genome. Man like any other organism adapts ecological changes slowly, generation by generation in gene complexes. The difference between man and other organism is that man is capable to steer his own evolution which other animals can't do. It is therefore said that a man can modified the role of natural selection by technological revolution. As an example eye cancer, the retinoblastoma is caused by dominant mutation, first develops in one eye and then spread to other eye and extends to brain and a child dies before he attains the adulthood. But today if the disease is diagnosed early it is possible to remove the tumour with the loss of affected eye and child can grow normal adult. Natural selection in normal course would eliminate gene from the population but if lethal conditions are to be completely cured in every patient, the frequency of the gene would increase slowly in the population.

Some scientists believe that there is deterioration in the genetic endowment of man due to improving conditions of life by modern medicines for example insulin allows diabetic genotypes to breed which was not possible in the past. The four different ways to improve the genetic endowment of man are: genetic counselling, genetic engineering, germinal selection and cloning. But methods like genetic counselling are quite desirable and genetic engineering techniques to correct the genetic defects. The human species will evolve genetically whether man interferes in the process or not. It is for the future generations to say whether man has acted correctly or not in steering his own evolution.

Q5. What is Eugenics? Mention the four ways through human genetic endowment may be improved.

Or

What attempts are being made to improve the genetic endowment of humans? **[June-2019, Q.No.-5 (b)]**

Ans. The science of improving a population and genetic stock of mankind by controlled breeding to increase the occurrence of desirable heritable characteristics.

Various eugenic processes and ways through which human genetic endowment may be improved such as:

- **Genetic counselling:** It is a practice, which informs prospective parents about the nature of a given condition that may exist in one of them or in the families and about the chance of its transmission in the offspring.

- **Genetic engineering:** It is a method of direct manipulation of genetic material. Genetic engineering techniques are developed to correct serious genetic defects, which are socially and ethically objectionable or unobjectionable and may have ethical and sociological implications.

- **Germ selection:** The germinal selection is a technique that involves the use of sperm and egg cells from individuals with desirable genetic constitutions through artificial fertilization.

- **Cloning:** It is a process that ensures that an offspring is a true genetic copy of an individual and it has been performed successfully in frogs and toads.

It appears that the future genetic evolution of man may depend on these procedures.

Question Papers

TAXONOMY AND EVOLUTION: LSE-07

December, 2017

Note: Question no. 1 is compulsory. Attempt any four questions from questions no. 2 to 6. All questions carry equal marks.

Q1. (a) Fill in the blanks in the following sentences:

(i) The system of scientific naming of organisms is termed as________ ________.

(ii) ______ deals with the study of fossil records of plants.

(iii) The evolution of cultivated plants has mostly been through ______ which is a source of variability in which the chromosome number changes to multiples of the ancestral diploid number.

(iv) The naturalist who thought of natural selection as mechanism of evolution at the same time as Charles Darwin did, was Alfred________.

(b) Expand any two of the following abbreviations:

ICZN, ICNB, ICVN

(c) Match the terms in Column A with those in Column B:

Column A	Column B
(i) Genera Plantarum	I. Geologic time scale
(ii) Paleocene	II. Bentham and Hooker
(iii) Naked seeds	III. Star fish
(iv) Echinodermata	IV. Gymnosperm

Q2. (a) Explain any five terms from the following:

(i) Taxon

(ii) Interspecific sterility

(iii) Key

(iv) Fauna

(v) Sexual dimorphism

(vi) Radioactive dating

(vii) Chemotaxonomy

(b) Write notes on any two of the following:

(i) Herbarium and its importance

(ii) Reproductive Isolation

(iii) Type specimens

Q3. (a) What are wildlife sanctuaries and what is their importance? Give the names and location of any two wildlife sanctuaries in India.

(b) Name the five kingdoms into which all organisms have been classified by Whittaker. Give the characteristics of any two of these kingdoms and an example of each.

Q4. What are variations? Discuss the importance of sexual reproduction in producing variations.

Or

What is industrial melanism? Explain by using the example of the peppered moth, Biston betularia.

Q5. Which geologic time period can human evolutionary history be traced to? What were the major trends in human evolution? Give the characters of Homo erectus.

Or

Explain Allopatric and Peripatric speciation highlighting the differences between these two modes of speciation.

Q6. Give an account of Homologous, Analogous and Vestigial organs with examples. Explain their roles as evidence of organic evolution.

Or

What is Numerical Taxonomy? State its principles. Also describe briefly the procedure adopted by Numerical Taxonomists.

It's possible to go on,
no matter how impossible it seems.
-*Nicholas Sparks*

TAXONOMY AND EVOLUTION: LSE-07

June, 2018

Note: Question no. 1 is compulsory. Attempt any four questions from questions no. 2 to 6. All questions carry equal marks.

Q1. (a) Fill in the blanks in the following sentences:

(i) The scientist who suggested Natural Selection as the mechanism of Evolution was________ ________.

(ii) Lamarck's theory on Evolution could not be accepted as ________ characters are not inherited.

(iii) The method by which the age of rocks and fossils can be estimated is ________ ________.

(iv) The binomial system of nomenclature was given by ________.

(b) Expand any two of the following abbreviations:

ICBN, IAPT, IUBS

(c) Match the terms in Column A with the ones in Column B:

Column A	Column B
(i) Coprolites	a. Zooflagellata
(ii) Flowers and fruits	b. Cyanobacteria
(iii) Anabaena	c. Fossil faeces
(iv) Trypanosoma	d. Angiosperms

Q2. (a) Explain any five of the following terms:

(i) Flora

(ii) Systematics

(iii) Vestigial organs

(iv) Phylogenetic classification

(v) Genus

(vi) Sympatric speciation

(b) Write notes on any two of the following:

(i) Co-evolution of Prey and Predator

(ii) Merits of Bentham and Hooker's System of Classification

(iii) Palynological Evidences as Tools of Taxonomy

(iv) Hybrid Sterility

Q3. (a) What does the geological time scale represent? Name the different Eras, Periods and Epochs in chronological order.

(b) What are Variations? Describe either mutations or genetic recombination as agents producing genetic variability in populations.

Q4. (a) What is the aim of setting up National Parks and Botanical Gardens? Write notes on any two National Parks of India.

(b) What are the different units or categories of classification? Arrange them in a hierarchical order. Define any three of them.

Q5. What is Speciation? How do the different types of isolating mechanisms facilitate speciation?

Or

In taxonomy, what is a "KEY"? List the different types of keys. How are they prepared and what are they used for?

Q6. (a) On the basis of fossil evidence, compare the characters of Homo erectus and Homo sapiens.

(b) Name the five kingdoms of organisms given by Whittaker. Give the characteristics of any two kingdoms. In which kingdom and phylum will you include (i) Fern, (ii) Euglena, (iii) Paramoecium, and (iv) Snail?

TAXONOMY AND EVOLUTION: LSE-07

December, 2018

Note: Question no. 1 is compulsory. Attempt any four questions from questions no. 2 to 6. Attempt five questions in all. All questions carry equal marks.

Q1. (a) Fill in the blanks:

(i) ______ and genetic recombination are the major sources of Variation.

(ii) ______ gave the system of binomial nomenclature for scientific naming of organisms.

(iii) ______ is a place for growing plants in a controlled environment.

(iv) An equipment called ______ is used for keeping freshly collected specimens.

(b) Choose the correct answer in any four of the following:

(i) The Great Banyan tree is located in ______. (Sibpur Botanical garden/Kew garden)

(ii) Bacteria and Cyanobacteria belong to the kingdom ______ (Plantae/Monera)

(iii) Flora of Delhi has been compiled by ______. (C.R. Babu/J.K. Maheshwari)

(iv) Vermiform appendix in humans is a ______. (Vestigial organ/Analogous organ)

(v) ______ is a place where dried and pressed specimens are classified and stored. (Herbarium/Museum)

(c) Match the items given in column A with column B:

Column A	Column B
(i) Fern	a. Arthropod
(ii) Exoskeleton	b. Mammals
(iii) Umbel	c. Type of Inflorescence
(iv) Hair	d. Prothallus

Q2. (a) Explain any two of the following terms:

(i) Genus

(ii) Omega Taxonomy

(iii) Karyotype

(iv) Hybrid sterility

(b) Write notes on any two of the following:

(i) Botanical Gardens

(ii) Wildlife Sanctuary

(iii) Numerical Taxonomy

Q3. (a) Why are field trips important for a plant taxonomist? What data does he/she collect during a field trip?

(b) Who proposed the 5 kingdom classification? Name the 5 kingdoms and give any one character and one example of each.

Q4. (a) What are the various types of evidences of evolution? Name them and explain any one of them in detail.

(b) What is Neo-Darwinism?

Q5. Write notes on any two of the following:

(a) Industrial Melanism

(b) Post-mating Isolating mechanisms

(c) Gene mutations

Q6. (a) Name the three mechanisms of speciation. Add a note on the mechanism related to geographical speciation.

(b) Describe the characteristic features of Homo erectus.

TAXONOMY AND EVOLUTION: LSE-07

June, 2019

Note: Question no. 1 is compulsory. Attempt any four questions from Questions 2-6. Attempt five questions in all. All questions carry equal marks.

Q1. (a) Fill in the blanks:

(i) Formation of new species from parent population is called ________.

Ans. Speciation

(ii) ________ ________ is the fundamental operating mechanism for organic evolution.

Ans. Genetic, variation

(iii) Aristotle started the work on ________ taxonomy.

Ans. Plant

(iv) Keys help in identification of ________ and ________.

Ans. plants, animals.

(b) Choose the correct answer in any four of the following:

(i) Kaziranga wildlife sanctuary is located in Jorhat, Assam/Calcutta.

Ans. Assam

(ii) The basic language of Scientific names is Latin/German.

Ans. Latin

(iii) The term flora/fauna of a place means the animals residing in that place.

Ans. fauna

(iv) Dioecious/monoecious plant means male and female flowers on the same plant.

Ans. monoecious

(v) The information carrying molecules in plants/animals are called semantides.

Ans. plants

(c) Match the items given in column A with column B:

Column A	Column B
(i) Naked Seeds	(a) Moss
(ii) Verminform appendix	(b) System of Classification
(iii) Benthm and Hooker	(c) Vestigial organ
(iv) Funaria	(d) Gymnosperm

Ans. (i) d, (ii) c, (iii) b, (iv) a

Q2. (a) Explain any two of the following:

(i) Neotaxonomy

Ans. Refer to Chapter-8, Q.No.-2

(ii) Fossils

Ans. Fossils are the remains or traces of ancient life that have been preserved by natural processes, from spectacular skeletons to tiny seashells. Imprints, tracks and trails can also become fossilised, like dinosaur footprints or worm burrows. These are called trace fossils. By studying the remains of life and the traces it left behind we can learn a lot about how animals and plants lived and behaved millions of years ago.

(iii) Lnterspecific sterility

Ans. Refer to Dec-2019, Q.No.-3(b)

(iv) Type specimens

Ans. Refer to Chapter-5, Q.No.-5

(b) Write notes on any two:

(i) Five Kingdom Classification

Ans. Refer to Chapter-3, Q.No.-5

(ii) Trends in Human Evolution

Ans. Before we further proceed to discuss the fossil history of the humans we shall briefly look into what distinguishes humans or genus Homo from his ancestors namely the apes. These differences are clearly indicative of the trends in human evolution which are to a certain extent supported by the available fossil evidence. Is it possible to specify certain criteria for assigning an organism to the family hominidae and the genus Homo? The answer to this question will also indicate certain definite trends in human evolution. Some of the general trends in human evolution which would often come into discussion even as this unit progresses are:

(1) The development of bipedalism so that the forelimbs are set free for performing specific tasks (Fig.).

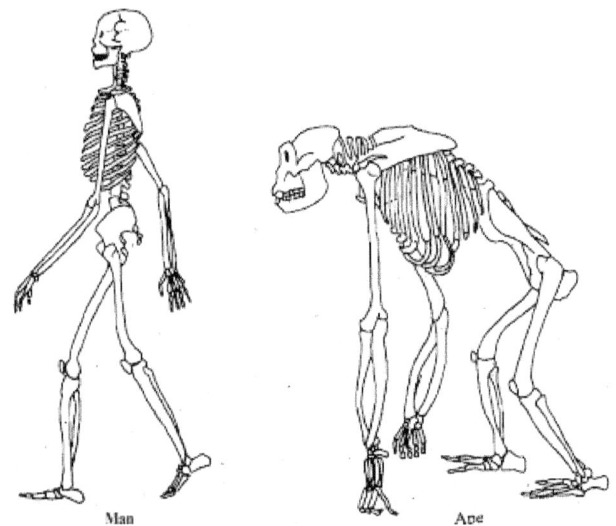

(2) The development of visual acuity which has been perfected by the evolution of a binocular stereoscopic vision.

(3) An increase in cranial capacity in order to accommodate a larger volume of brain (Fig.).

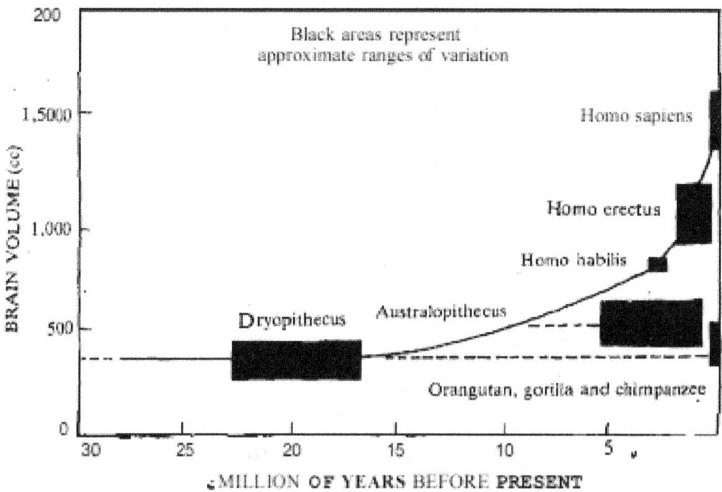

(4) A receding forehead.

(5) Development of opposable thumb (Fig. below).

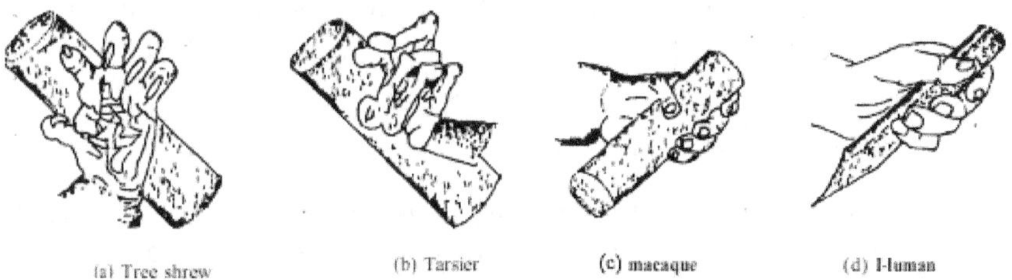

(6) The development of arched feet. Along with the above mentioned anatomical changes other important factors that were responsible for delimiting the genus Homo are:

(i) Evolution of culture by which it is meant that individuals in a society formulate concepts and communicate them to the other members of the society;

(ii) By communication it is meant that language has to be developed as a fundamental medium of culture.

In subsequent sections, our analysis of human evolution would focus the trends we mentioned above in relation to fossil records. Whereas it is possible to obtain the .f fossil evidence for the anatomical traits we mentioned and to a certain extent to depict cultural evolution, the language is not a fossilizable one. We shall briefly discuss later in this unit and more elaborately in the next unit the evolution of communication skills in human societies.

(iii) Principles of Binomial Nomenclature

Ans. Refer to Chapter-4, Q.No.-3

(iv) Botanical gardens.

Ans. Refer to Chapter-5, Q.No.-3

Q3. (a) What is a key? How are keys prepared and what useful purpose do they serve for a taxonomist?

Ans. Refer to Chapter-6, Q.No.-2

(b) Discuss the modern trends in taxonomy and discuss the use of electrophoresis in it.

Ans. Modern taxonomists consider that the gross morphological characters are not always sufficient to provide means of differentiation in determining the genetically and evolutionary relationship between taxa. To achieve this the taxonomical evidences from anatomy, embryology, palynology, cytology, palaeobotany, ecology, biochemistry etc. are discussed.

Dr. V. Puri has said "One of the most significant modern trends in plant taxonomy is towards a synthesis between the older methods, outlook and more recent developments in our knowledge of plants".

Bailey (1949) has said, if a truly natural classification is to be attained, it must be based upon "the analysis and the harmonisation of evidence from all organs, tissues and parts".

Morphology in Relation to Taxonomy: Gross morphology has no doubt provided the foundation and framework for taxonomy, but it has become increasingly clear that contributions to systematics may come from almost any branch of biology. The modern taxonomist has, therefore, to have a broader outlook than his predecessor does a few years ago.

Morphology is the study of structure and form of plants, usually dealing with the organism and its component organs:

Morphology has been the most widely used tool in the classification of higher plants from a very long time. Botanists and taxonomists in various classes of plants have so extensively studied morphological features that it might be said that there is little left to learn.

According to modern concepts, however it is not correct. Practically all the herbaria systems of classifications, botanical manuals are based on comparative morphology and anatomy.

Morphological characters are traditionally useful as evidence at all taxonomic levels, but particularly at the specific and generic ranks. Morphological evidence provides the basic language for plant characterisations, identification, classification, and relationships. Generally, morphological data are easily observable and obtainable, and thus most frequently used in taxonomic studies.

Morphological characters are plants habit, root structural types, stem habit, stem structural types, bud structural types, leaf structural types, inflorescence types, flower types, perianth structural types, androecial types, stamen types, gynoecial types, carpel types, ovule types, fruit types and seed types.

Modification of flowers in stamen number, another position, ovary position, style length, stigma shape, number of carpels, number and fusion of perianth parts etc., contribute to the reproductive success of the species. The growth habit (herbaceous or woody) of plants may be of primary usefulness in classification. Brassicaceae and herbaceous; Asteraceae have both woody and herbaceous members.

Electrophoresis: Electrophoresis is the motion of dispersed particles relative to a fluid under the influence of a spatially uniform electric field. Electrophoresis of positively charged particles (cations) is sometimes called cataphoresis, while electrophoresis of negatively charged particles (anions) is sometimes called anaphoresis.

The electrokinetic phenomenon of electrophoresis was observed for the first time in 1807 by Russian professors Peter Ivanovich Strakhov and Ferdinand Frederic Reuss at Moscow University, who noticed that the application of a constant electric field caused clay particles dispersed in water to migrate. It is ultimately caused by the presence of a charged interface between the particle surface and the surrounding fluid. It is the basis for analytical techniques used in chemistry for separating molecules by size, charge, or binding affinity.

Electrophoresis is used in laboratories to separate macromolecules based on size. The technique applies a negative charge so proteins move towards a positive charge. Electrophoresis is used extensively in DNA, RNA and protein analysis.

(c) Expand any two of the following:

(i) ICZN

Ans. International code of zoological Nomenclature

(ii) IAPT

Ans. International Association of plant Taxonomy

(iii) ICNCP

Ans. International code of Nomenclature

(iv) ICBN

Ans. International code of Botanical Nomenclature

Q4. (a) What is coevolution? Explain with the example of coevolution of prey and predators or of plants and herbivores.

Ans. Refer to Chapter-12, Q.No.-3

(b) Name the three types of Natural Selection and write a few sentences on any two of these.

Ans. Stabilising Selection: This type of natural selection occurs when there are selective pressures working against two extremes of a trait and therefore the intermediate or "middle" trait is selected for. If we look at a distribution of traits in the population, it is noticeable that a standard distribution is followed:

Example: For a plant, the plants that are very tall are exposed to more wind and are at risk of being blown over. The plants that are very short fail to get enough sunlight to prosper. Therefore, the plants that are a middle height between the two get both enough sunlight and protection from the wind.

Directional Selection: This type of natural selection occurs when selective pressures are working in favour of one extreme of a trait. Therefore when looking at a distribution of traits in a population, a graph tends to lean more to one side:

Example: Giraffes with the longest necks are able to reach more leaves to each. Selective pressures will work in the advantage of the longer neck giraffes and therefore the distribution of the trait within the population will shift towards the longer neck trait.

Disruptive Selection: This type of natural selection occurs when selective pressures are working in favour of the two extremes and against the intermediate trait. This type of selection is not as common. When looking at a trait distribution, there are two higher peaks on both ends with a minimum in the middle as such:

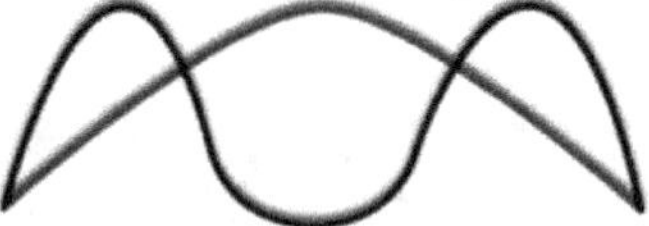

Example: An area that has black, white and grey bunnies contains both black and white rocks. Both the traits for white and black will be favored by natural selection since they both prove useful for camouflage. The intermediate trait of grey does not prove as useful and therefore selective pressures act against the trait.

Q5. (a) Define species and speciation. Describe one mechanism of speciation.

Ans. Refer to Chapter-13, Q.No.-1 and Q.No.-2

(b) What attempts are being made to improve the genetic endowment of humans?

Ans. Refer to Chapter-15, Q.No.-5

Q6. (a) Distinguish between Homologous and Analogous organs. What is a Vestigial Organ? Name a vestigial organ in humans.

Ans. Refer to Chapter-10, Q.No.-10 and Q.No.-4

(b) Give a brief account of evolution of horse.

Ans. Refer to Chapter-10, Q.No.-12

❑❑❑

TAXONOMY AND EVOLUTION: LSE-07
December, 2019

Note: Attempt five questions in all. Question no. 1 is compulsory. Attempt any four questions from question no. 2 to 6.

Q1. (a) Match the items given under column A with those given under column B:

Column A	Column B
(i) Numerical Taxonomy	(a) Baron Cuvier
(ii) Scolex	(b) Assam
(iii) Kaziranga Wildlife	(c) Tapeworm Sanctuary
(iv) Comparative Anatomy	(d) M. Adanson

Ans. (i) d, (ii) c, (iii) b, (iv) a

(b) Define the following terms:

(i) Taxon

Ans. Refer to Chapter-1, Q.No.-2

(ii) Aneuploidy

Ans. Refer to Chapter-11, Q.No.-6

(iii) Fossils

Ans. Fossils are the remains or traces of ancient life that have been preserved by natural processes, from spectacular skeletons to tiny seashells. Imprints, tracks and trails can also become fossilised, like dinosaur footprints or worm burrows. These are called trace fossils. By studying the remains of life and the traces it left behind we can learn a lot about how animals and plants lived and behaved millions of years ago.

(c) Fill in the blanks in the following statements by choosing the correct alternative from the words given within brackets:

(i) _________ is the Father of Taxonomy. (R. H. Whittaker/Linnaeus)

Ans. Linnaeus

(ii) _________ measures selection pressure (Progressive selection/selection coefficient) in any genotype.

Ans. selection coefficient

(iii) Coevolution between plants and herbivores often develops into _________ relationship. (Altruism/mutually beneficial)

Ans. mutually beneficial

Q2. (a) List Von Baer's four principles of embryonic differentiation.

Ans. Refer to Chapter-10, Q.No.-7

(b) With help of an example, discuss how action of natural selection is influenced by the changing environment.

Ans. Refer to Chapter-11, Q.No.-7

Q3. (a) Name Whittaker's five kingdoms of organisms and list their characteristics.

Ans. Refer to Chapter-3, Q.No.-5

(b) Distinguish between interspecific sterility and hybrid-sterility.

Ans. Interspecific Sterility: In interspecific sterility, the failure in mating occurs because of inability of the sperm to reach the egg in animals and the pollen to reach ovules in plants. In plants interspecific crosses usually result in the non-growing of the pollen tubes or the slowing down of the growth. If pollen from another species is transferred to a plant along with the pollen from conspecific individuals, the growth of the pollen tube of the latter is much faster than the former and all the fertilisation is conspecific.

In certain cases of interspecific crosses the pollen tube begins to grow but then bursts ensuring that no fertilisation occurs. Such an event occurs when the chromosome number of the male parent is higher than female parent. For instance, three specie: of tobacco plants are known to occur: Nicotiana tabacum, N, sylvestris and N. tomentosa. N, tabacum has 48 chromosomes and the other two species have 24 each. Probably N. tabacum is a tetraploid produced by a cross between the other two species. A cross between either of the two species and N. tabacum is successful only if the latter is used as a female parent. In such a cross the style tissues have 48 chromosomes and the pollen tube has only 12 chromosome, giving a ratio of 4 : l. When the cross is between N. sylvestris and N. tomentosa, the style tissue of both the species has 24 chromosomes and the pollen tube has 12 chromosomes giving a 2 : l ratio. But if N. tabacum were to be a male parent, and the either of the other two species a female, then the style tissue has 24 chromosomes and the pollen tube has 24 chromosomes giving 1 : l ratio. It is only under these circumstances, that is when the ratio is close to 1 : l the bursting of pollen tube occurs. It is assumed that a high osmotic pressure in the pollen tube causes it to burst and that this trait is controlled by a gene. Essentially a genetically coupled physiological mechanism prevents interspecific crosses in the tobacco plant.

There are other instances where a zygote may be formed but its further development may not occur beyond a stage. Thus in interspecific crosses of jimson weed plant, the embryo dies around the eight cell stage. In the case of hybrid plants, it is believed that there is an inadequate nutritional relationship between the developing embryos and the endosperm resulting in the death of the embryos.

The genetic basis of interspecific sterility is not clearly understood in many cases. Yet, one good example comes from studies on the tropical fish of the genus Xiphophorus. X. maculatus (moon fish) carries a dominant gene (Sd) responsible for a dark spot on its dorsal fin. The gene produces macromelanophores which are potential tumors. In a closely related species X. helleri (swordtail), the gene occurs in recessive form (sd). A cross between the two species produced fertile F_1, offspring. The hybrid offspring has the heterozygous genotype Sdsd and in such a condition the fins are more heavily pigmented than the homozygous (SdSd) genotype. The Sdsd progeny always have lethal tumors. A backcross of Sdsd fish with the recessive genotype (sdsd) have shown that half the progeny have lethal genotype (Sdsd). Thus in Xiphophorus interspecific sterility manifests in the form of production of offsprings with lethal genes in them.

Hybrid Sterility: Hybrid sterility can be regarded as yet another form of interspecific sterility. The offspring of the interspecific crosses are mainly sterile. Geological studies have shown that the chromosomes of the hybrid individuals fail to synapse at the time of meiosis and thus result in either non-production of gametes or defective gametes. Unless the chromosomes of parents are accurately separated which might result in viable gametes,, in most cases the gametes are not produced and if produced they may not be fertile. The commonly cited example is the mule, a sterile animal the product of a cross between a donkey and a horse. Further, the hybrid species in general are found to have grossly abnormal reproductive system. If normal reproductive system is present, then meiosis is abnormal and non-viable gametes are produced.

Thus various types of reproductive isolating mechanisms are at work in different groups of organisms to maintain the distinctness and uniqueness of species.

Q4. (a) Discuss the major trends in evolution of the genus Homosapiens.

Ans. Refer to Chapter-14, Q.No.-3

(b) What is 'radioactive dating'? How does it help in the study of evolution?

Ans. Refer to Chapter-10, Q.No.-1

Q5. (a) Describe merits and demerits of Bentham and Hooker's classification of seed plants.

Ans. Refer to Chapter-2, Q.No.-2

(b) Discuss the importance of Operational Taxonomic Units (OTUs) and character selection in Numerical Taxonomy.

Ans. Numerical methods in taxonomy are not new. Simple statistical methods like standard deviations, t-tests and chi-squared have been used for several years. Recently with development of electronic digital computers, numerical analysis of a large quantity, of taxonomic data in a relatively short period of time has become possible. This has led in the last twenty years to the development of a new branch of taxonomy called numerical taxonomy or taxometrics.

The computation of data by evaluating numerically the affinity or similarity between organisms and then ordering them into taxa takes very little time, probably a few seconds. However, the preparation of the data in a suitable form for input into the computer is a very tedious task requiring painstaking examination and recording of information.

The use of computers in numerical taxonomy has made it possible to compare a large number of characters from many organisms with relative ease. After comparisons of the organisms they are grouped according to overall similarity or dissimilarity and wherever necessary presented graphically.

The number of characters studied in numerical taxonomy are usually about 50-100 from approximately the same or greater number of organisms.

The term organism in this field refers to individuals, populations, specific genera or any other taxonomic category and so far this reason they are generally called as 'operational taxonomic units' or 'OTUs'.

The different conditions in which the identification characters occur are known as 'character state'. A particular organ may be absent or present, functional or non-functional. In such simple cases they are said to be 'two state characters'.

Many traits, however, exhibit a number of possible states and so are termed as multistate characters. Both two state characters and multistate characters may be qualitative or quantitative. Now let us see the stepwise manner in which numerical data is prepared and analysed.

The very first step in numerical taxonomy is to decide the OTUs to be studied.

(1) Then the characters to be used for studying the OTUs are selected. Usually a large number of characters are taken as it is presumed that the greater the number of characteristics the more valid the classification.

(2) The characters chosen include any observable attribute or trait of the OTUs: morphological, behavioural, ecological embryological etc. All such traits have to be observable phenotypic characters and so it is for this reason that the resultant grouping, classification or key obtained from taximetric is said to be phenetic. In other words, it is not based on evolutionary or phylogenetic or phyletic relationships. All the selected characters are given equal weightage. Thus each character is of the same value as the other.

(3) Once the characters are selected they have to be recorded in a suitable form.

This process is called coding. Quantitative attributes like the number **of** lips in the nematodes, or measurements of parts of the body can be recorded directly. Two state or multistate characters need to be coded. In the case of two state characters the presence is usually coded as 1 or + and absence as 0 or -.

(4) When a character exists in more than one qualitative state, these may be broken down into a series of two state characters. For example, the cuticle of an insect may be white, yellow, brown or black, the character can be coded + or 1 when 1 present or -,or0 when absent for each state in turn. Or each of the possible states can be indicated by a number and the disagreement or agreements (usually termed mismatch or match) can be recorded as + or - for each comparison between OTUs.

(5) An alternative method would be to use multistate coding where a single trait can be coded in a number of states, each being represented by

a numerical symbol or code e.g, 1, 2, **3** etc. depending on the range of variation. Thus if **we** again look at the colour of the cuticle of an insect, we can assign different code to different colours such as white = 1, brown = 2, black = **3,** and so on, Besides qualitative characters such as colour of hair, cuticle etc, multistate coding is also useful in quantitative characters such as number of lips, setae, length of body, width of body, number of markings and other characters involving measurements. **A** code is prepared for the range of variation as for example, body length may be coded as 5-10 **mm** = 1, 11-15 mm = 2, 16-20 mm = 3, 21-25 mm = 4 etc. Occasionally due to some reason or another no comparison is possible or data may be missing **for** one of the traits of the OTUs. Such situations are coded as NC (no comparison).

(6) Now the next step after the OTUs have been selected and the character states and their subsequent coding has been determined is the presentation of data in the form of a primary data matrix or txn matrix where 't' represents the OUT's and **'n'** the characters Fig. 8.28a and 8.28b.

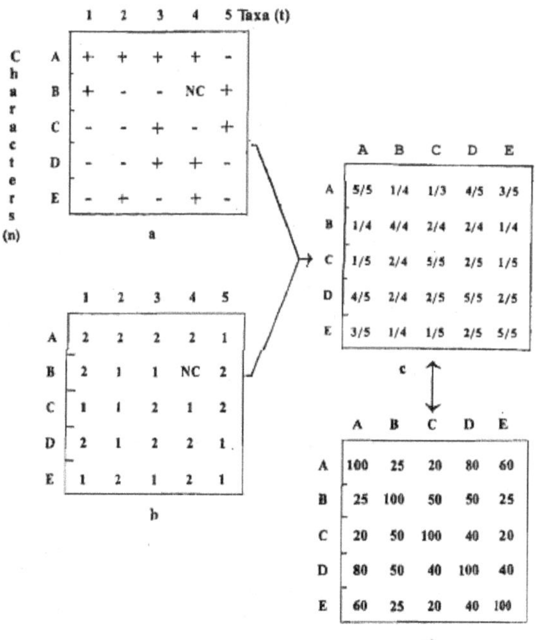

If we have studied 50 OTUs and scored 100 characters from each, then we will obtain 50 × 100 = 50,000 Units of information. Thus the large amount of information obtained make the use of computers usually absolutely necessary in numerical taxonomy.

(7) Now, in the next stage, each **OTU** is compared in turn with all the others with respect to their character states (Fig. 8.28). In order to accomplish this there must be some means of, comparing the degree of similarity. This is achieved by calculating the coefficient of similarity (S) $S = $ **m/n.** Here, m is the number of matches of character states between pairs of OTUs, and n is the total number of characters (NC entries are excluded). The coefficient of similarity is presented as you can see in Fig. 8.28 c & d in a tabular form in a similarity matrix in which each OTU is compared with every other one.

The coefficients of similarity for OTUs are indicated as fractions (Fig.c) or more usually, however, in decimal fractions or percentages (Fig.d & 8.29). In Fig. 8.29 we have chosen a hypothetical similarity matrix of 10 OTUs (A-J) (n) and their corresponding observable characters 1-10 (t).

TAXON (OTUS) (n)

	A	B	C	D	E	F	G	H	I	J
A	100	53	80	63	62	82	50	83	50	60
B	53	100	55	57	57	55	86	56	87	56
C	80	55	100	62	64	85	51	86	50	62
D	63	57	62	100	74	63	54	65	56	96
E	62	57	64	74	100	64	56	67	56	72
F	82	55	85	63	64	100	54	87	52	65
G	50	86	51	56	56	54	100	54	85	65
H	83	56	86	63	67	87	54	100	54	67
I	50	87	50	56	56	52	85	54	100	55
J	60	56	62	96	72	65	65	67	55	100

TRAITS (t)

(8) Let us see how the coefficient of similarity is calculated in percentage. Consider, the OTUs **A** and B in Fig. 8.28c. You will observe that one out of a total of 4 of its characters match so the similarity between them will be 1/4 × 100 = 25 per cent. Obviously 100 per cent would mean that the two groups are identical with respect to the characteristic chosen and 0 per cent means they are totally different. The type of numerical taxonomic analysis described here is the simplest of a large number of possible techniques and is known as 'single linkage cluster analysis' in which the measure of similarity is based on match/mismatch. In Fig, 8.29 as we mentioned before we have chosen a hypothetical similarity matrix worked not in percentage of l0 OTUs (A-J) and their corresponding observable characters 1-10' (t) in order to explain to you how the measure of similarity is further worked out by the single linkage cluster analysis.

(9) You will observe that the figures on the upper and lower sides of the diagonal line in Fig. 8.28d and 8.29 are mirror images. So it is customery to illustrate only one part as we have done **in** Fig. 8.30.

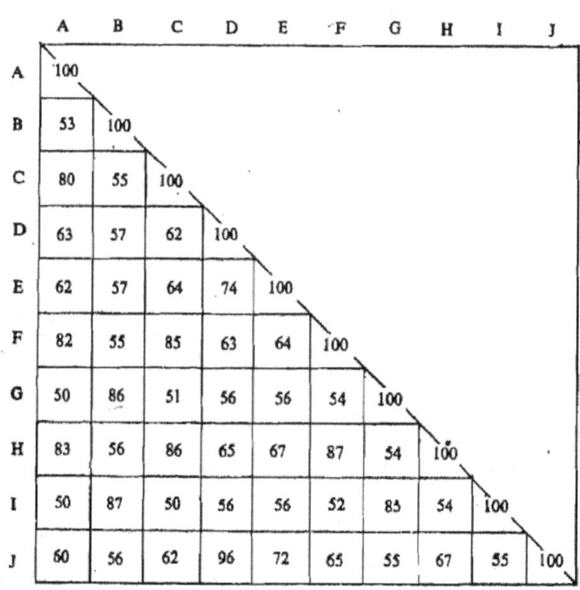

	A	B	C	D	E	F	G	H	I	J
A	100									
B	53	100								
C	80	55	100							
D	63	57	62	100						
E	62	57	64	74	100					
F	82	55	85	63	64	100				
G	50	86	51	56	56	54	100			
H	83	56	86	65	67	87	54	100		
I	50	87	50	56	56	52	85	54	100	
J	60	56	62	96	72	65	55	67	55	100

(10) Now, the next step involve the rearrangement of the similarity matrix so that the groups of OTUs which show closest similarity are

clustered together. Again several techniques are available for doing this. However, with the small numbers of OTUs and their correspondingly small number of characters, chosen by us, **it** is possible by just looking at Fig. to observe immediately a high degree of similarity between **ACF** and H, between D E and J and again between B, G, and I. So, the matrix can be organised to form blocks of high similarity as indicated in Fig.. Usually however the date of the similarity matrix to very large and so blocks of ligh similarity can only be calculated with the help of computers.

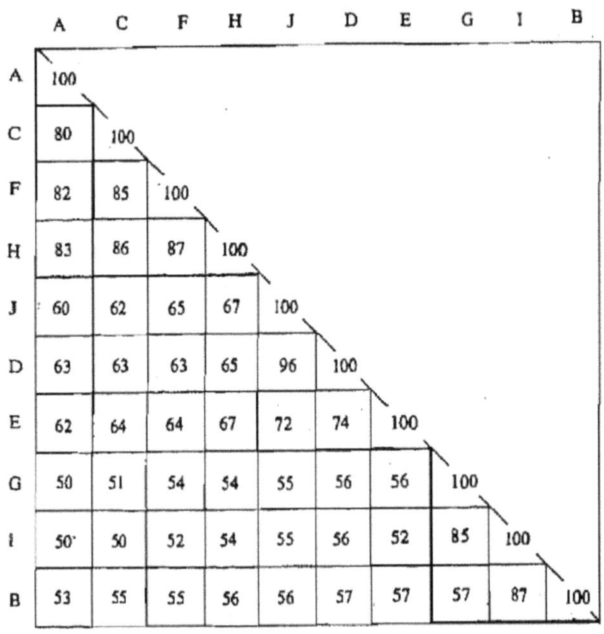

	A	C	F	H	J	D	E	G	I	B
A	100									
C	80	100								
F	82	85	100							
H	83	86	87	100						
J	60	62	65	67	100					
D	63	63	63	65	96	100				
E	62	64	64	67	72	74	100			
G	50	51	54	54	55	56	56	100		
I	50	50	52	54	55	56	52	85	100	
B	53	55	55	56	56	57	57	57	87	100

(11) The blocks of similarity in Fig. are based on the percentage of shared character states and can be represented graphically in the form of a tree or dendogram known as 'phenogram' (Fig.). In this type of data presentation, the phenetically similar OTUs can be linked together by horizontal lines drawn at appropriate distances in relation to a vertical scale, which represents degrees of similarity and which, as you can see, is expressed in percentage. The clearly evident clusters of similar OTUs are termed as 'phenon' and the levels which indicate

the degree of similarity on the vertical scale are known as phenon lines.

In the hypothetical dendogram (Fig.), the OTUs **A, C, F** and H form a phenon which have a similarity of 80-87% D and J have 96% similarity end both are joined to E at about 70% level. G, I and B are joined at 85-87% level. The group formed by *J*, D and E is linked to **A, C,** F and H at 60% phenon line. More distant from all of these seven are *G* I and B to which they are linked with only 50-57%, similarity,

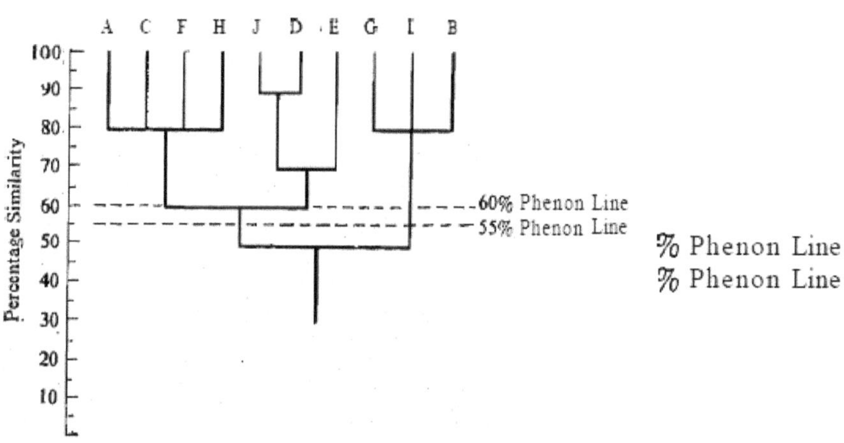

It is quite tempting though not justifiable to regard such dendograms as phylogenet or at least approximations to them. It is mainly because of this and because of the subjective nature of categories, such as genus, subfamily, family etc, that levels **of** phenon lines have been used to delimit taxa above the species level. For instance,. phenon with about **70%** similarity may be regarded as of generic rank and those **of** say 50% **of** family rank. 'This provides an obvious though arbitrary method of standardising the level of various categories in the taxonomic hierarchy. Whether or not genera and family should be delimited in this manner by more or less constant levels of phenon lines is a, debatable points.

Many other techniques **of** numerical taxonomy are available now, some with special objectives.

Classification based on the methods of numerical taxonomy almost certainly have some phyletic component as they result to some extent from similarities due to common ancestry.

As mentioned before, usually no 'a priori' weighting or extra weightage is given to characters employed in numerical taxonomy. However, once the procedure outlined above have been completed and a classification constructed, it is then possible to reconsider the characters used and to determine which are good characters. That is, which are constant and highly correlated with other characters. These characters are then given special weighting in the diagnosis of taxa and identification with the help of keys. Such weighting is said to be 'a posteriori' or 'correlation' weighting.

The development of computer techniques in numerical taxonomy, have been proved useful for various other applications such as in key construction automatic identification programs, in storage and retrieval of taxonomic data and in studies on evolutionary pathways.

Q6. Write short notes on any two:

(a) Taxonomic hierarchy

Ans. Refer to Chapter-3, Q.No.-3

(b) Biological concept of speciation

Ans. Refer to Chapter-13, Q.No.-1

(c) Homologous organs

Ans. Refer to Chapter-10, Q.No.-10

(d) Chemotaxonomy

Ans. Refer to Chapter-7, Q.No.-6(d)